The Atlas of

NEW HAMPSHIRE PONDS

2nd
Edition

northern
Cartographic

MAPPING · PUBLISHING

Northern Cartographic, Inc. is a Vermont based mapping and publishing company which produces quality maps and atlases available for purchase by the public, maintains a retail map store with worldwide coverage and provides custom cartographic services. For further information contact:

Northern Cartographic, Inc.
4050 Williston Road
South Burlington, Vermont 05403
(802)860-2886

Cover design: Kevin Ruelle, Ruelle Design & Illustration
Photographs courtesty of: American Museum of Fly Fishing,
Manchester, Vermont

Permission to reproduce, in any form, any part of the material in this publication requires written permission from the publisher.

ISBN 0-944187-33-1

Introduction to the Second Edition

Northern Cartographic is pleased to offer this Second Edition of the Atlas of New Hampshire Trout Ponds. The contents have been updated and revised to reflect the current status of New Hampshire's "trout pond" fishery. Several ponds have been deleted and a number of new ponds have been added. The most significant change has been combining the former two volumes into a single book.

We continue to be indebted to the large numbers of researchers whose work on New Hampshire's lakes and ponds formed the foundation of this book. In addition to the bibliographic citations, specific appreciation must be extended to the agencies and individuals who have generously helped us in putting this book together.

We are grateful for the assistance of the New Hampshire Safety Services Division of the Department of Safety; both the Forest and Land and Parks and Recreation Division of the Department of Resources and Economic Development; the Office of Travel and Tourism Development; the Department of Transportation, Bureau of Transportation Planning and System Management and the New Hampshire State Library.

We also want to thank the following individuals for their assistance in compiling a variety of information: Jeffrey Schloss, Lay Lakes Monitoring Program, New Hampshire Cooperative Extension; Julia Dahlgren, Sea Grant Extension, University of New Hampshire; Paul Dent, Fish and Game Department; Ken Warren, Weed Watcher Program, Department of Environmental Services; and Betsy McCoy Poirier, The Loon Preservation Committee.

We owe a special thanks to Rachael Albert for assisting with cartographic revisions and to Carl Blumberg for his meticulous editing of the accompanying text. We also are grateful for the generous cooperation of Alanna Fisher, American Museum of Fly Fishing, for her help in researching and providing the photographs included in this volume.

We would like to thank Jack Clausen of the University of Vermont's School of Natural Resources and Jim Kellogg of the Vermont Department of Water Resources for the basic text on acid rain; and most especially Robert Estabrook with the Biology Bureau of the New Hampshire Department of Environmental Services for his contribution on the "acid rain" status of New Hampshire's trout ponds.

For the first edition research, we once again would like to recognize the New Hampshire Fish and Game personnel whose field work was incorporated into the book. This list includes Carl B. Ackerley of Newington, William Hastings of Gorham, Brian A. Howe of Rumney, Peter Lyon of Melvin Village and Kenneth P. Warren of Peterborough.

Within the New Hampshire Fish and Game Department we are especially grateful to Donald Miller, Fisheries Biologist, New Hampton and Scott Decker, Fisheries Biologist, Lancaster for their able assistance in the review and update of ponds in their regions.

In this present work, as with the first, we are most grateful to Charles Thoits, Senior Biologist, New Hampshire Fish and Game Deparment for his generous cooperation in reviewing and updating the current material.

Table of Contents

The Trout Ponds

A satisfying sense of serenity comes from returning year after year to fish our favorite places. For people who love to fish for trout, a lake or pond is a permanent feature on the landscape. While the catch may vary, we depend on the lakes themselves being there for our return visits. That granite shoal which held willing trout last spring will be there next spring and for a lifetime of springs to come. Yet in geologic time, measured in thousands of lifetimes, lakes and ponds are among the most fleeting features on the face of the land. As soon as they are created they begin to fill in. Hundreds of lakes and ponds now dotting the New Hampshire landscape owe their character and, in many cases, their origins to the work of ice.

During the last ice age, snow accumulated over several centuries around Hudson Bay encouraging a continent-sized sheet of ice. Nurtured by an extended period of wet and cold the ice sheet grew and moved outward and southward under its own crushing weight. Eventually a continental glacier covered all of New England so thickly that even Mt. Washington (6,288 feet high) lay buried. Several glacial advances and retreats are theorized with the most recent glacier still melting in parts of New Hampshire only about 12,000 years ago.

As it melted away, the revealed landscape had been radically altered. There were no trees or soil; the first few feet of bedrock had been planed away. In the succeeding vegetations even the bare tundra was hundreds of years away. Many of the existing lakes had been gouged deeper and wider. Others had been wiped away. Melting ice provided such immense quantities of water that nearly all of our present-day lakes and ponds were considerably larger. Winnipesaukee's Alton Bay, for example, was nearly four times its current area and extended more than two miles south of New Durham.

New lakes were created both by gouging and damming
as glacial deposits and huge blocks of stagnating ice dis-
rupted developed lines of drainage. Such conditions formed
some mammoth lakes. One, glacial Lake Hitchcock, filled
the entire Connecticut River Valley from Middletown, Connecticut, northward to Lyme, New Hampshire. Lake Hitchcock
is believed to have lived between two and four thousand
years, breaching its dam about 10,000 years ago. Many
larger river valleys held glacial lakes, notably Lake Merrimac,
Lake Contoocook, and Lake Upham (in the Upper Connecticut Valley). The city of Keene now occupies the floor of what
was Lake Ashuelot, another glacial lake.

The abundant lakes and ponds in New Hampshire are
only a remnant of a staggering number during the post-
glacial thaw. In addition, individual lakes have undergone
an evolutionary process.

After formation (or alteration) by glaciers, a lake was
cold and barren. Cold temperatures and little decaying
organic matter made oxygen plentiful. Such lakes are called
oligotrophic. They were poor food producers. Examples of
this type in its archetypal form are seen in high barren cirque

lakes found above treeline in the Rocky Mountains. All New Hampshire lakes were once this type. As time passed sedimentation and increased vegetative growth mitigated the brutal environment. Shallow areas yielded food-producing zones while depths stayed relatively free of organic matter. While they remain cold and highly oxygenated, such lakes (still classified as oligotrophic) are ideal habitat for lake trout and other cold water species.

As the water body matured, increased organic growth continued. In New Hampshire, as the glacial age waned, climatic warming increased water temperatures and accelerated the process. In time, many of the state's ponds became such rich producers of organic material that during the summer the oxygen supply would be depleted by decaying organic matter. These types of water bodies are called "eutrophic". The name means "good food", but from the angler's point of view it is something of a misnomer. The process of eutrophication results in a change from cold water species to warm water fish which demand less oxygen.

This natural evolutionary process has been complicated by human intervention. Some lakes and ponds in this book are man-made. Most have had their natural levels raised by damming. Through the introduction of pollutants humans have accelerated the eutrophication process. Some lakes and ponds only maintain their trout populations by careful human management. Many, however, still have self-sustaining populations and, barring catastrophe, will sustain them for centuries to come.

In recent years, we have witnessed the devastation in the high lakes of the Adirondacks and it has become increasingly clear that acid rain could represent such a fundamental catastrophe.

Acid rain knows no political boundaries. In the United States and Canada the present debate centers on identifying the location of the major producers of these acidic pollutants and how much are generated. Two primary contributors of sulfur dioxides are the tall smokestacks of fossil-fuel burning power plants in the Great Lakes and the smelters of the International Nickel Company (INCO) plant in Sudbury, Ontario. Both nations produce nearly half of the nitrogen oxides by motor vehicles on their highways and in the great Eastern cities.

These pollutants mix with water vapors in the upper atmosphere to form sulfuric and nitric acids which then likely travel hundreds of miles in easterly flowing upper wind currents before falling as acid rain and acid snow. Acid precipitation causes irreversible damage to lakes and ponds. Individuals must educate themselves about this problem and respond at the ballot box.

For this book's purposes a lake or pond is called a "trout pond" if trout live in it. Private, no trespassing, or no public access ponds were eliminated from consideration. Also not included were so-called "kids' ponds" or "derby ponds" stocked for youngsters, and some experimental waters managed by the Fish and Game Department.

Beaver ponds are also not included. The beaver pond has a near-mythical reputation for hot fishing, some of it is deserved. Beavers have made a comeback in New Hampshire. Virtually extinct by the 1830's, their works are now found throughout the state. Most beaver ponds are no larger than an acre. Without intervention by stocking, there is a definite cycle to their fishing quality. In the first year or two, increased forage and the protection of deeper water may produce fish of a larger size. Sedimentation, however, is generally rapid and in a short time the gravel needed for spawning is covered by silt. Vegetation inundated by the pond eventually dies and its decay may deplete the supply of oxygen. The result is a rapid drop-off in the quality of fishing. Beaver ponds are almost exclusively brook trout water. Prime beaver ponds are best located by exploration.

Fishing Strategies

The fish population of a lake is never uniformly distributed throughout the water body. Various concentrations of fish are found here- and- there in a changing (and sometimes predictable) pattern. Their location in the lake at a given time is determined by identifiable factors, the presence of food and suitable habitat as most basic. The physical features of a lake considered with these factors will suggest some of the ways the charts may be used in planning a fishing strategy.

The largest or greatest numbers of fish necessarily don't inhabit the middle or deepest part of the lake. In fact, except for the constraints of water temperature, relatively shallow water can also attract concentrations of fish. "Shallow water" can be defined many ways but let us consider it as 20 feet deep or less. This region of the lake includes the so-called "littoral" zone. Here light penetrates to the bottom and allows rooted plants to grow. In some New Hampshire shallow lakes, this zone covers the entire water body. In others it may be a narrow band along the edge of the lake due to a rapid drop-off to very deep water. Turbid, darkly colored water may also limit the penetration of light. The littoral zone is the food producing region of the lake. Insects, crustacea and forage fish are abundant here. If temperature permits, trout and salmon will be found in this part of the lake. Islands, reefs and shoals rising out of deeper water may create littoral zones "in the middle" of a lake. Generally speaking, however, the food-producing zone of a lake is along its perimeter.

The inlets and outlets of a lake also are places where food and therefore fish concentrate. The food is washed in by feeder streams or slowly drawn together by the pull of the outlet. The actual affected area of the lake will vary from several to tens of thousands of square feet depending on size and velocity of the current. Inlets, with their heavier currents and cold oxygenated water, are more productive fishing grounds.

Seasonal migration for spawning is another factor that makes the shoals and perimeter of a lake the places where trout congregate. Brook trout move shoreward in the fall. In late October they build their redds in the gravel of an inlet or use the detritus, twigs and bark found in the lake itself. Lake trout also spawn in the fall. Spawning time has seasonal variation but is usual from mid- to late October. The lake trout does not build a redd but deposits its eggs over bouldery shoals in one to four feet of water. Classic hot spots for lake trout include windswept, rocky reefs which rise abruptly from deep water or the shoals just off an island. Land-locked salmon migrate inshore in early October. They actually spawn two weeks or so later. Salmon seek out gravel beds of the inlets and outlets of a lake in which to build their redds. Brown trout spawn from October onward. Rainbows are the only resident trout which spawn in the spring. In April and May they will be found coming and going from the gravel beds of a lake's inlets and outlets.

As a source region for food and a location involved in the breeding cycle, we would expect to find trout in the shallow waters of a lake. With all the excellent reasons to fish a lake "at its edge", why bother leaving shore to fish deeper water? In this part of North America there are four good reasons at least: June, July, August and the first few weeks of September.

Trout and salmon demand cold and highly oxygenated water. Starting from ice-out, temperatures rise. As water warms, less oxygen can remain dissolved in it. During the week or two after ice-out the water is cold enough to keep all of our salmonids happy. Each species has specific temperature requirements that determine where they can be found. As water temperature rises and the water begins to give up its oxygen, trout and salmon retreat to the reservoir of cold water in deeper parts of a lake.

The lake trout demands the coldest water. Its ideal water temperature is a chilling 50°F. The lake trout is the first to leave shallow water. In New Hampshire this species is confined to large deep lakes that maintain a quantity of cold, oxygen-rich water even in summer's doldrums. In spring, just after ice-out, lakers may be taken in the frigid shallows on light spinning tackle or streamer flies. During summer, lake trout will be found at depths where the water is 65°F or colder. Generally this means depths of 40-100 feet or more. Fishing them during this time is most effectively done by deep trolling with lures that imitate forage fish.

Land-locked salmon is the next species to leave the lakes' shallow waters. During April, May and into June they may be taken "up top" by casting or trolling lures and flies. They prefer water temperature in the mid-50s. A recent study showed that during the summer most salmon are found in depth of 40-70 feet, while this fish rarely is taken in depths of 100 feet or more. Three-quarters of salmon's diet is made up of forage fish - significantly smelt. Encouraging to the fly fisherman, the remaining 25% of their diet is insects.

The brook trout has an optimum temperature range between 57°F and 61°F but can be found in lakes and ponds with water temperatures exceeding 68°F. During the dog days of summer (August) this fish retreats to a pond's deeper colder water but during the balance of the season may be taken near the surface. The brook trout is more responsive to diurnal temperature changes than lake trout or salmon and will establish a pattern of feeding in the evening and early morning as summer progresses. Brook trout eat mostly insects. The worm remains the favorite bait with an undeniable rate of success.

Brown trout prefer temperatures ranging from 54°F to 60°F, but tolerate temperatures over 80°F. They eat a varied diet; insects, mollusks, crayfish and forage fish. Once they grow larger, they rely heavily on smaller fish. Very large browns may eat nothing else. More than any other trout, brown trout are nocturnal feeders.

The rainbow trout thrives best in 65°F to 68°F waters and tolerates temperatures over 80°F. When the water temperatures drop below 70°F the rainbow swims to the surface. As a lake's surface temperature rises to 70°F or more, this fish finds a level with temperatures nearer 60°F. The rainbow's feeding pattern also is related to diurnal fluctuations in temperature as the season heats up. Rainbows are believed to be less of a daytime feeder than the brook trout. The rainbow eats insects, crustaceans and forage fish. Large rainbows, like the brown trout, may rely primarily on forage fish.

Individual characteristics of each lake and pond and variation in seasonal weather from year to year prevent accurate prediction of temperature at a given depth. On-site readings with a minimum-registering thermometer is the only surefire method of determination. Understanding the general dynamics of water in a lake, however, can lead to reasonable guestimates or can assist a search with a thermometer. Water is densest and therefore heaviest at 39.2°F. When water warms from this temperature it expands and becomes lighter. Surprisingly enough, water also expands when cooled below 39.2°F. This singular expansion before freezing causes very cold water to float. Lakes and ponds therefore will freeze from the top down rather than from the bottom up, a fortunate natural quirk without which New Hampshire's lakes would freeze solid in the winter thawing only partially in the summer. This property of water, coupled with seasonal variation in climate, make possible the identification of four stages in the temperature distribution cycle of a deep lake: winter stagnation, summer stratification and two periods of overturn, in the spring and in the fall.

In winter a lake is locked in ice and entirely isolated from the outside environment. In winter stagnation lakes demonstrate a vertical temperature series in which the coldest water is floating on top, just below the ice, at a temperature just above freezing. As one descends the water a relatively abrupt rise in temperature occurs until the water reaches its maximum density at around 39°F. Below this all the water remains at 39°F. This type of layering, once achieved, maintains a steady state until ice-out.

The spring turnover comes shortly after ice-out. Surface waters are quickly warmed above 32°F. As they are warmed up toward 39°F they sink. This process, aided by the wind as mixing agent continues until all the lake reaches 39°F. Once the whole lake reaches 39°, and all its water

reaches the same density, it is possible for the wind to circulate and overturn the entire mass of water in the lake.

As warm weather continues, water temperature rises above 39.2°F. Now warmer water floats on top. In the early part of spring this layer of warm water is thin and periodically broken by wind and wave action. As summer progresses, however, distinct layers or strata of temperatures result. In summer stratification three characteristic layers of water exist: a warm upper layer, a cold bottom layer and a narrow zone or band in which a rapid transition occurs between the warm and cold layers. This zone of rapid transition is called the "thermocline". In this zone, water temperatures drop very gradually to minimum readings. Minimum temperatures will vary but in deep lakes would consistently hover in the low 40s. While stratification maintains itself, virtually no water is exchanged between upper and lower layers. In the dead of summer catching trout means penetrating below the thermocline to cold water. Generally speaking, the thermocline begins at depths of 15-25 feet. In very darkly colored water it may begin only a few feet below the surface.

In fall the process of lake turnover is repeated. Surface waters are cooled and sink until they reach their own temperature (density) level. This continues until the whole lake is at the same minimum temperature and the entire water mass can be easily mixed by the wind.

The presence of springs is a local factor of tremendous importance in determining where trout will situate themselves. These occur in many of our lakes and ponds. Some shallow water bodies maintain their trout populations by the cold water of these springs. In a small lake or pond, midsummer temperatures may make these spring areas the only place where the fish are free of temperature stress. In such cases, springs will create localized areas of lake bottom thick with trout while the balance of the water body has none. Finding one of these cold water pockets is another on-site task done with a thermometer. In midsummer, even in relatively shallow ponds, the exchange of water between top and bottom is diminished. Thus surface water temperatures may offer little clue to the location of the springs.

A good rule of thumb to judge the significance of springhole feeding within a given lake or pond is to compare the volumes of its inlets with its outlets. If more water appears going out than coming in, then springs are a significant feature of the lake. Springs may occur as seepage along a lake or pond's edge and can be detected by thermometer readings a few feet from shore. Such springs may be visible as wet or darkly colored ground just back from the edge of the pond. Springholes may also occur hundreds of feet into the lake's interior with the cold (heavy) water flowing down underwater hillsides or bubbling up from the bottom to collect in pools. In the heat of the summer, at dusk or in early morning, trout may feed in the surface above these springs, returning periodically to the cold water to rest.

Having found one of these pockets of cold water you will want to note its location for a return visit. A good way to mark any kind of fishing hot spot some distance offshore is to line yourself up using four points as shown in the figure. Try to choose lines of sight that are at right angles to each other. There is considerable leeway on the angle but the important thing is to choose identifiable landmarks and record them so they are not forgotten. This book would be a good place to list the information.

Locating Your Fishing Spot

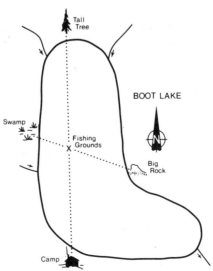

New Hampshire and Acid Rain

Acid rain was first scientifically documented in Sweden about 25 years ago. Since then hundreds of "dead" and "dying" lakes in Scandinavia have been attributed to its effects. Now a body of evidence seems to indicate that scores of lakes in New York's Adirondack Mountains may be sharing the same fate. New Hampshire too, receives acidic precipitation at a rate that may be detrimental to sensitive bodies of water. Although few New Hampshire lakes are known to be fishless, water chemistry suggests stressful conditions and impacts on the food chains of trout in approximately half of the state's lakes and ponds.

What Is Acid Rain?

Sulfur dioxide and oxides of nitrogen resulting from the combustion of fossil fuels are the two major precursors to acid rain. Sources of these pollutants include coal and oil fired electrical generating plants, smelting and other industrial operations. Roughly 50% of the nitrogen oxides in the United States are emitted from motor vehicles. In northeastern United States, most researchers agree that the major component of acid rain is sulfur compounds which form sulfuric acid and account for 65% of the acidity in precipitation. Nitrogenous oxide compounds which form nitric acid are the second major component, accounting for 30% of the acidity in precipitation. Sources of these gases may also be natural, including lightning, volcanic eruptions and decaying plants and animals. Nevertheless, cultural sources are the most significant producers of acid rain pollutants in New England.

During the late 1960's towering smokestacks were designed and constructed to reduce regional pollution levels. They successfully reduced localized pollution, but larger, more-widespread problems were created. Winds dispersed airborne pollutants over greater distances resulting in the formation of acid rain.

During transport, these pollutants come in contact with cloud moisture, sunlight and humidity and through a series of complex chemical reactions form dilute solutions of sulfuric and nitric acid. Sophisticated trace studies indicate that at least 75% of the sulfate in rain and snow falling in the Northeast originates from the industrialized Ohio River Valley.

These acids come back to earth in rain, snow, sleet or even fog. Some gases and particles fall from the atmosphere without any type of precipitation occurrence, and later combine with surface water to form acids.

Measuring Acid Rain

A rain sample's acidity is measured on a scale of 1 to 14 called the pH scale. A value of 7 is neutral. Values below 7 are acidic and values above 7 are basic. The pH scale is logarithmic, which means that a unit change on the pH scale is a tenfold change in acidity. For example, a pH of 4 is 10 times more acidic than a pH of 5, and 100 times more acidic than a pH of 6. It also means that the amount of acid rain required to reduce pH increases tenfold for each unit decrease in pH. At pH 7, only .9 µeq/L of hydrogen ions are needed to reduce the pH one unit to 6. At pH 5, a unit decrease to pH 4 requires 90µeq/L of hydrogen ions.

The pH Scale

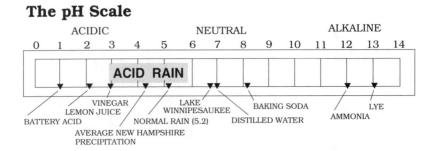

The pH of "Normal" Rain

Moisture exposed to the atmosphere will combine with carbon dioxide (CO_2) in the atmosphere to form a weak carbonic acid. Since distilled water saturated with CO_2 has a pH of 5.6, natural, unpolluted rain is often said to have a pH of 5.6. However, other natural sources of both acid and basic materials exist. In most areas, including New Hampshire, more acid materials predominate and unpolluted "normal" rain has a pH below 5.6, probably 5.0 to 5.2.

Acid Rain in New Hampshire

The acidity of precipitation in central and south central New England has been monitored respectively by the Hubbard Brook Experimental Station in Thornton since 1963 and by the New Hampshire Department of Environmental Services in Concord since 1972. The median annual pH for precipitation currently falling in New Hampshire (1989) is 4.2 to 4.4. This is approximately 10 times more acidic than "normal" rain, depending on the value used for "normal" (approximately 5.2). This reduction in the pH of the precipitation is caused by large amounts of acid. Only 6.2 µeq/L of hydrogen ions are required to bring distilled water at pH 7.0 down to "normal rain's" 5.2 pH. Another 56.8 µeq/ L are needed to reach the 4.2 pH of the precipitation currently falling on New Hampshire. High elevation areas are particularly affected by acid rain because of greater rainfall at elevation and because the areas are bathed often in acid fog.

Acid Status of New Hampshire Lakes

The New Hampshire Department of Environmental Services monitors the acid status of the state's lakes through a variety of programs. A systematic inventory of lake and pond water quality, both winter and summer, was begun in 1975. This was supplemented in 1982 with a program developed with the Fish and Game Department to annually sample selected remote, high elevation ponds by helicopter. A volunteer lake assessment program also contributes to the data base.

The Department has recent data (as of April 1993) for 592 lakes and ponds in New Hampshire. Using the summer, epilimnetic (upper water level) samples, the state's lakes are classified below, based on both alkalinity and pH.

Alkalinity Classification of New Hamphshire Lakes

Sensitivity Classification	Alkalinity (mg/L)	Number of Lakes	Percent	Area (acres)	Percent
Acidified	≤ 0	14	2	396	< 1
Critical	0.1 - 2.0	96	16	9,363	6
Endangered	2.1 - 5.0	195	33	41,231	26
Highly Sensitive	5.1 - 10.0	188	32	95,204	60
Sensitive	10.1 - 20.0	80	14	11,633	7
Not Sensitive	> 20	19	3	871	< 1
		592	100%	158,698	> 99

pH Classification of New Hamphshire Lakes

Sensitivity Classification	pH (Units)	Number of Lakes	Percent	Area (acres)	Percent
Acidified	< 5	14	2	516	< 1
Critical	5.0 - 5.4	27	5	2,393	2
Endangered	5.5 - 6.0	76	13	6,259	4
Satisfactory	> 6	474	80	146,630	94
		591	100%	115,798	100%

"Alkalinity" measures the buffering capacity of a lake, (its ability to accept acid inputs without changing its pH). It is often called ANC or Acid Neutralizing Capacity. The alkalinity of a lake is determined primarily from the underlying bedrock. The granitic bedrock found in Hew Hampshire lacks buffering materials, resulting in lakes with low buffering capacity. About 85% of the state's lakes are highly sensitive or worse (alkalinity of 10 mg/L or less).

The actual acidity of a lake also is measured by pH. While only 2% are acidified (pH <5), 20% have pH values low enough to impact some of the biota (pH of 6 or below). Photosynthesis by plants during the summer growing season can artificially increase the pH. If winter pH values are used, nearly half of the lakes have pH values of 6 or below.

The classifications include lakes throughout the state, including those subject to urban or agricultural runoff which tends to counteract acid rain impacts. If only remote ponds are evaluated, the situation worsens. Fully 95% of the remote ponds are at least highly sensitive (alkalinity of 10 mg/L or less) and two-thirds are endangered (pH of 6 or less). High elevation lakes tend to be the most vulnerable to acid rain for a number of reasons, including greater rainfall, small watersheds, no upstream lakes, little or no soil cover over the bedrock, and more acid fog.

Trends in the acid status of New Hampshire lakes are also alarming. Data collected from over 700 lakes by the Fish and Game Department, primarily in the late 1930's, demonstrated that 9 lakes had alkalinities of less than 2 mg/L and 2 lakes had pH values below 5. Using recent data discussed above on fewer (592) lakes, 96 lakes had levels below 2 mg/L and 14 lakes had pH values below 5. Although analytical methodologies have changed through the years, the number and magnitude of the changes demonstrate that New Hampshire lakes are being adversely impacted by acid rain.

Effects on Aquatic Organisms

Low pH in a pond endangers fish in two ways. First, acidity can reduce the amount of food available to fish. Second, acid waters can directly harm the fish.

When the pH of water is decreased from pH 6 to pH 5, several changes are seen in the aquatic food pyramid. The type of algae found shifts from the free floating types to those that attach themselves to rocks. Some water plants die and acid-loving sphagnum moss begin to appear on the bottom. Less bacteria survive to decompose plant debris. More fungi appear. At pH 6, some of the freshwater mussels begin to disappear. At a pH of 5.5, there are fewer mayflies. Below 5.5, crustaceans die. Even short-term exposure of these animals to acid has been found to cause lethality. No snails are found in water below pH 6.0. But air-breathing organisms, including the whirligig and water boatman, survive very well in highly acid waters and might be an important source of food in acidified ponds.

Studies on the directly harmful effects of acid waters on fish have been made both in fish tanks and by inventory in the natural setting. Fish show symptoms, much like we do, when subjected to acid-induced stress; they begin to hyperventilate and "cough". Other effects include slower growth rates. At a pH of 5 or below, there is mortality of both trout eggs and fry. There have been reports that female trout cannot release their eggs at this low pH. Remember that one of the spawning seasons (rainbows/steelheads) is in the spring and is triggered by the same snowmelt that can produce "pH shock".

Waters more acid than pH 5 are lethal to trout. Rainbow trout are more sensitive to acid waters than browns. Brook trout are least sensitive. Generally, second-year fish resist acid stress more than first-year fish.

How does acid affect fish? Studies to date indicate at least two ways that acid waters harm fish. First, acid waters usually (but not always) have less dissolved minerals and the salt balance in fish gets upset by acidification. Second, some heavy metals and aluminum that occur naturally in water become very mobile and toxic in acid waters. Some studies show that maximum toxicity occurs at pH 5. The aluminum in the water causes a mucous clogging of the trout's gill which prevents adequate respiration.

Conclusion

The extent of damage to aquatic organisms in New Hampshire's lakes and ponds caused by acidic precipitation is unknown primarily because of the scarcity of detailed biological studies of aquatic organisms besides adult fish. The damage can be estimated indirectly, however, by using current chemical data and general relationships between pH and aquatic organisms observed at lakes that have been studied biologically. As discussed in the previous sections, biological impacts begin at approximately pH 6. Organisms in approximately half of the state's lakes are exposed to pH values of 6 or less. Although game fish are not directly impacted at this pH, key elements of their food chain are eliminated. It is important that chemical monitoring continue and that biological studies enlarge our data base on existing conditions and trends, and to document improvements as sulfur and nitrogen oxide emissions are reduced in the United States.

For further information on the water quality of lakes and ponds in New Hampshire, please contact:

Department of Environmental Services
Water Supply & Pollution Control Division
Biology Bureau
6 Hazen Drive, PO Box 9
Concord, NH 03301

This section on acid rain is based on a similar report in The Atlas of Vermont Trout Ponds, written by John C. Clausen, Ph.D. of the University of Vermont and James H. Kellogg of the Vermont Department of Water Resources. The original section was updated and substantially revised for New Hampshire lakes and ponds by Robert H. Estabrook, Chief Aquatic Biologist of the New Hampshire Department of Environmental Services.

Responsibilities

Early town histories and the back pages of 19th Century newspapers commonly report about one or two individuals catching and dressing a few hundred trout on a Sunday afternoon. The environmental conditions and "pioneer ethic" that could support this behavior have passed. Plenty of good fishing still remains in lakes and ponds as the result of careful management. Access itself is maintained by State and Federal purchases or negotiations with the private owner. In many cases access is allowed by landowners with no formal agreement, but it is contingent upon individuals acting responsibly. Respect for Fish and Game Regulations and private property are basic requirements which contribute to the continuation of a valuable resource.

An increase in environmental awareness among anglers has resulted from both the problems involved with stepping into the 21st Century and the realization that the "fishing experience" is not just measured by the size of the catch. Clean water and relatively undisturbed natural areas serve a vital recreational purpose by allowing us an opportunity to feel closer to nature. We all are responsible for preservation of these resources by both supporting conservation efforts and by personal behavior.

Fish and Game Regulations

Purchase of an annual fishing license by both residents and non-residents is required. "Where, when and how" of fishing are governed by the New Hampshire Department of Fish and Game which annually publishes a booklet of regulations. Open and closed seasons for trout, designated trout waters, methods of angling, limits on weights and numbers of fish, minimum lengths, species identification, special regulations (such as ice fishing) and waters with reduced limits are a few of the subjects covered. Changes in the regulations occur annually and it is incumbent on the angler to know the current law. The booklets are generally available where licenses are purchased (sporting goods outlets, general stores, etc.). Fish and Game regulations may also be obtained by writing:

New Hampshire Department of Fish and Game
2 Hazen Drive
Concord, NH 03301

Private Property

If we can maintain a tolerant atmosphere, or, hopefully increase the amount of land open to public use, respect for private property must become a priority. Some landowners who post their land grant permission for fishing on an individual basis. It is well worth asking. Fishing on private property is illegal without permission and hurts the case for opening up areas not presently open to public use. All signs indicating no trespassing should be obeyed.

Littering

An important part of the outdoor experience is appreciating solitude in an unspoiled setting. This feeling is difficult to maintain when confronted with someone else's trash. The proliferation of disposable packaging and synthetic materials has yielded litter which takes lifetimes to degrade, if it degrades at all. Leave nothing behind but footprints and pack out all the "found trash" you can carry.

Parking

Whenever possible park in a designated parking area. New Hampshire law requires that a car parked along a highway must have all four wheels off the traveled portion of the road. Never park as to block the access to a side road or private drive. Parking is prohibited on the New Hampshire Interstate system. Parking which meets these conditions generally is available near where you want to fish or at the trailhead.

Motorboats

The laws regulating the use and registration of motorboats are to be found in a free booklet entitled New Hampshire Boating Laws, Rules and Regulations. Write:

State of New Hampshire
Department of Safety
Hazen Drive
Concord, NH 03301

Here are some tips on safe boating:
- It is recommended that all boaters, and certainly children and non-swimmers, wear an approved vest-type flotation device for their added safety.
- Recreational boats must carry a readily accessible Coast Guard- Approved Personal Flotation Device for each person on board.
- Boats must keep a distance of 150 feet from shore, other boats, rafts, docks, swimmers, unless pro - ceeding at headway speed.
- Fire Extinguishers are required on all motorboats.
- All boats must be equipped with lights if operated at night.
- When boating on an unfamiliar body of water or for long periods, leave a float plan with someone for your protection.
- Straddling the bow, sitting on the transom, and sitting on the gunwales are prohibited.
- It is strongly urged that all boats give way to very large vessels whose maneuvering and stopping ability is limited. Those who maliciously or carelessly

create a hazard to navigation through their actions in relation to other boats may have their privilege to operate suspended.

- The weather in the lakes regions can change quickly. At the first sign of threatening weather, seek shelter.

The Timberlands of the North

A number of trout ponds in northern New Hampshire are located on lands owned by timber companies. Champion International is the most prominent of these companies. Their policy of recreational use states:

"(Champion International) lands are for the most part open to the public for day use. No overnight camping is permitted, nor are campfires.

"Roads may be closed by the company when in use of logging operations; when vandalism to equipment or lease camps becomes excessive; and during mud season. At times a road might be closed at night only, in which case the time of closing is posted on the gate.

"Since these roads are heavily used by log trucks and both Company and contractor vehicles, all vehicles should be operated in a cautious manner, with operators alert at all times to the possibility of meeting other vehicles in tight situations. Parked vehicles should be well off the travelled portion of the road."

Loons

Up to the present the call of the loon has been held synonymous with North Country lakes. Its future in New Hampshire, however, is very insecure. Nesting loon populations are currently half historical numbers and the state legislature has classified the bird as a threatened species.

The Common Loon is a nearly goose-sized diving bird living on the lakes of the northern United States and Canada. They are most often recognized by their calls which sound like wild laughter or yodeling. On the water they are observed swimming and diving. Often they swim with only their heads sticking out of the water. In diving they will disappear for seemingly long periods, reappearing some distance away. Most studies show that loons feed primarily on "trash" fish and thus benefit the sports fishery.

The loon is threatened because of human encroachment. Anglers may contribute to this bird's demise by frightening adults off the nest or scattering and separating parents and young when approaching in a boat. Consumable litter - even food litter in trash cans - can have indirect negative effects, it feeds raccoons which increase predation on loon eggs or nestlings.

The Loon Preservation Committee is responsible for the statewide recovery effort. One tactic has been to build artificial nesting islands. These are rafts generally built of four cedar logs and hardware cloth, and planted with shoreline plants and mosses, then positioned to resemble a small natural island on which loons are likely to nest. These rafts help the loons avoid the effects of raccoon predation and water fluctuation. They should be left undisturbed.

For further information on this work (primarily volunteer help), write

The Loon Preservation Committee
PO Box 604
Moultonborough, NH 03254

THE CRY OF THE LOON—

NO LAUGHING MATTER

The Common Loon is quickly becoming Uncommon on many of our Lakes. **YOU** can help ensure a future for this remarkable bird.

PLEASE

•Protect Loons and their chicks when boating by not chasing them.

•If you suspect Loons are nesting in any area, leave them in peace.

•Steer Away from Loon family flocks.

(HINT: If you are boating near shore and a Loon appears from nowhere and starts splashing and calling, you are probably too near its nesting or chick rearing site.)

LOONS ARE FULLY PROTECTED BY STATE AND FEDERAL LAWS.

For more information about the habits and history of the Loon in New Hampshire, please write or call:

 THE LOON PRESERVATION COMMITTEE

(A Project of the Audubon Society of N.H.)

The Northern New England Zebra Mussel Watch

The zebra mussel is a bivalve, freshwater mollusk that originated in eastern Europe. Since its discovery in the great lakes in 1988, it has spread to other North American waters including Lake Champlain. The adult mussel is typically less than two inches long with alternating dark and light bands on its shell. The mussels grow in clusters, attaching themselves to objects with strong threads. The veligers (larval form) are free-swimming and nearly invisible. The zebra mussel can clog industrial and public drinking water intakes; foul boat hulls and engine cooling systems; and disrupt aquatic ecosystems.

Boaters can inadvertently transport zebra mussels from infested waterways. If you have been boating in Lake Champlain or other fresh water outside of New England, it is important to take the following precautions before launching your boat in New Hampshire waters:

- Remove any vegetation attached to your trailer.
- Flush your engine cooling system, bilge areas and live wells with tap water.
- Discard old bait and bait water.
- Leave boat out of water to dry for at least 48 hours.
- If it is visibly fouled with algae, leave it out until the exterior is completely dry or the hull has been washed at a car wash.

For additional information on the zebra mussel watch contact:

Sea Grant Extension
Kingman Farm
University of New Hampshire
Durham, NH 03824

or

New Hampshire Lakes Lay Monitoring Program
Pettee Hall
University of New Hampshire
Durham, NH 03824

THE ZEBRA MUSSEL is a bivalve mollusk that was probably introduced into North American waters from Europe through the discharge of ballast water from oceangoing ships. Since its discovery in the Great Lakes in 1988, the zebra mussel has spread to other freshwater systems. It colonizes hard surfaces and clogs power plant, industrial and public drinking water intakes; fouls boat hulls and engine cooling systems; and disrupts aquatic ecosystems.

Most adult zebra mussels are thumb-nail size, but they can grow larger. They usually have light and dark bands on their D-shaped shells, but their patterns vary. They grow in clusters, attaching firmly to substrates with strong adhesive threads. If you think you've found some, please contact one of the organizations listed below.

Boaters can inadvertently transport zebra mussels from infested waters into uninfested lakes and waterways. Mussel larvae can be carried in boat bilge water, live wells, bait buckets and engine cooling systems. Juvenile and adult mussels can "hitchhike" attached to boat hulls, engine drive units, boat trailers and aquatic vegetation clinging to any of these. Adult zebra mussels in moist shaded areas (in bilges or inside trailer frames, for example) can live for several days out of water.

STOP the zebra mussel

You can help prevent the infestation of our lakes and rivers by following these guidelines. If you've been boating in fresh water outside of New England, please don't put your boat in our waters until you:

- Remove any vegetation attached to boat or trailer.
- Flush engine cooling system, bilge areas and live wells with tap water.
- Discard any old bait and bait bucket water.
- Leave boat out of water to dry for at least 48 hours. If it is visibly fouled, leave it out until the exterior is completely dry or you've washed it at a car wash.

For more information on the zebra mussel menace, contact Sea Grant Extension, Kingman Farm/UNH, Durham, N.H. 03824 (603/749-1565) or the New Hampshire Lakes Lay Monitoring Program, Pettee Hall/ UNH, Durham, N.H. 03824 (603/862-3848).

The Eurasian Water Milfoil Threat

Eurasian water milfoil (Myriophyllum Spicatum L.) is an aquatic plant that has become an economic and recreational nuisance in increasing numbers of New Hampshire lakes and ponds. This plant is known for its rapid growth and spread. Commonly found in shallow bays and along the shoreline. It forms dense weed beds that can reduce seriously the availability of spawning grounds, displace beneficial native plants, impair fishing and other recreational uses of water bodies and otherwise alter a lake's natural environment.

The growth and spread of this plant is a threat to all of New Hampshire's lakes and ponds because once established, there is no known way to eradicate it. Milfoil can be managed only by a variety of expensive and time-consuming means.

Anglers can help prevent the spread of Eurasian water milfoil by taking care not to transport plant fragments from one water body to another. These are most commonly transmitted on boats and trailers as they are moved from lake to lake. Boats and trailers should be carefully inspected before leaving the launch sites. Take special care to remove all plant fragments from the trailer hitch, rollers and axle, as well as the boat's bottom, motor, propeller and wet well. Interested parties may obtain detailed information from:

Department of Environmental Services
6 Hazen Drive
Concord, NH 03301

Milfoil currently exists in many of the protected coves and bays of Lake Winnipesaukee. It is also found in Lees Pond, Moultonboro, Crescent Lake, Wolfeboro, Paugus and Opechee Bays, Laconia, Contoocook Lake, Jaffrey, Flints Pond, Hollis, and Turkey Pond, Concord. Anglers should be especially vigilant and exacting in cleaning their rigs before leaving these water bodies.

BOATERS!

WEED OUT STOWAWAYS

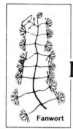

Fanwort

STOP
NUISANCE WEED
SPREAD

Milfoil

Aquatic weeds are often found

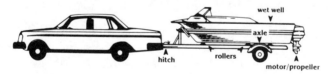

wet well

axle

hitch   rollers

motor/propeller

Remove & Dispose

NEW HAMPSHIRE DEPARTMENT OF ENVIRONMENTAL SERVICES
BIOLOGY BUREAU
P.O. BOX 95 — HAZEN DRIVE
CONCORD, NH
Tel. 603-271-3505

A Word About Getting There

The maps presented in the Atlas have been produced expressly as fishing guides. They are not complete general maps of the area shown. In their research and production, a number of cartographic sources were employed. These sources include: State of New Hampshire General Highway Maps, U.S. Geological Survey quadrangles, aerial photographs, a number of unpublished private sketch maps and some published maps and trail guides. Although we feel our own renderings are meticulous representations, they do not replace topographic maps, compass and common sense.

A handy supplement to this book is the New Hampshire Official Highway Map. It is available free at rest areas on the Interstate Highway, local information booths, or by writing:

Office of Travel and Tourism Development
PO Box 856
Concord, NH 03301

With few exceptions all roads on this map are driveable during the fishing season. This certainly is not the case with many roads that lead to the backwoods ponds. Frequently these are seasonal roads with no guarantee of passability even for four-wheel drive vehicles. Spring is the worst season for travelling on unpaved roads. Remember that in the mountains and in parts of the North Country "spring conditions" can linger into July. Local weather, of course, can wash out a road at any time of year. Use good judgment. When in doubt, ask or check conditions ahead on foot. In the end, if doubt persists, park the car and walk the extra distance.

The Backwoods Ponds

For those intrepid anglers who will be satisfied with nothing less than New Hampshire's remote foot-access ponds, some special consideration is warranted. Although becoming truly lost is a rare occurrence, finding some of these ponds, even with the help of this guide, is not always easy. The trails involved have a wide range of quality. Some, like the Appalachian Trail, are well-marked and see quite a bit of use. Others are nothing more than overgrown logging roads that sometimes become difficult to follow. We strongly recommend use of U.S.G.S. Topographical Maps and a compass when hiking to these ponds. These maps are inexpensive and can be ordered directly from the U.S.G.S. or purchased from local distributors such as mountain shops or bookstores. The current price of $2.50, when ordering direct from the government, is a true bargain. When ordering write:

Branch of Distribution
U.S. Geological Survey
Box 25286
Denver, CO 80203

To order you need to supply the name of the state, the series, and the name of the quadrangle. For the convenience of the reader, the index at the back of this book contains the name and series of topographic maps for all the trout ponds accessible by foot trails only. For those who are unfamiliar with route finding and map use there are a number of excellent books on the subject. Some of these are listed in the bibliography. You can also check your local library catalogue under "Orienteering," "Map Reading", or "Map".

For your guidance when fishing, we strongly recommend reading these publications:

Camping and Hiking on the White Mountain National Forest-A short description of the weather, facilities, and requirements for hiking, campgrounds, and backpack camping.

Rules and Regulations Regarding Permit Systems in

the White Mountain National Forest Wilderness Areas
    Your Hike in the White Mountain National Forest - A
short guide for hikers and campers, how to choose a route,
learning to live with the mountains, regulations.
    Fishing in the White Mountain National Forest - A
description of mountain ponds, species of fish, and location.

    All of these publications can be acquired free of charge by
writing:

Forest Supervisor's Office
White Mountain National Forest
PO Box 638
Laconia, NH 03246

Publications can also be picked up at any one of five
Ranger Stations located in Plymouth, Bethlehem, Conway,
Gorham and Bethel. Experienced hikers know the limits of
their physical ability and stay within them. The mountains
can be as unforgiving as they are beautiful. Weather conditions, which can change rapidly, post the greatest danger to
the hiker. Do not underestimate the need for proper protec-
tive clothing and staying well fed. It is surprising but true
that hypothermia (exposure) claims most of its victims when
the air temperatures are in the 40s and 50s. Rain, wind, and
physical exhaustion can turn a day trip to a trout pond into
a life-threatening situation. Mental disorientation, a symp-
tom of hypothermia, can make the closeness of civilization
largely irrelevant. Good raingear, warm clothing, and an
oversized lunch will make your hike more enjoyable, and
offers a margin of safety.
    The backwoods pond offers the angler a special world
of fishing. Many of these places combine healthy trout
habitat with low fishing pressure. The result is often fast
action and good- sized trout. More importantly, some reclu-
sive hours spent in an unspoiled environment and the
opportunity to see wildlife in its natural setting provide us
with a deeper appreciation of nature's wonderfully delicate
balance. In going to these places we can leave behind, if only
for a little while, the cares and complexities of contemporary
living. We return, with or without trout, a little richer for the
experience.

Using and Interpreting the Atlas

The maps in this book have been arranged by "scanning" the state from west to east, starting in the north and working south. Each page of the atlas contains three maps and a chart. In the upper left of the page is a small outline of New Hampshire which contains a black rectangle. This rectangle represents the area covered by the larger map and shows its location in the state. In the upper right of each page is a Regional Access Map. On the map small stars show the approximate location of trout ponds. The area covered by the larger map is shown by means of a rectangular outline.

The larger map on each page is the "Local Access Map". This map shows the location of trout ponds by larger stars, and gives the detailed road and trail networks needed to find the ponds.

To find a particular pond, look up the name of the pond in the index which will give you the page number on which the pond is mapped.

The legend which precedes the main body of maps is, for the most part, self-explanatory. There is a need, however, to comment on and to define some of the terms used in the charts which appear at the bottom of the pages.

Access Rights - Refers to property ownership of land immediately adjacent to the ponds. In cases where information regarding this was not available it is indicated by a dash.

Brook, rainbow, brown trout, etc. - Refers to the presence of a designated species as determined by 1993-1994 data supplied by Fish and Game Department personnel. A blank space in the chart means that a species is not believed to be present.

Boat Access - A blank space indicates that there is no boat access. An undeveloped boat access is one that is designed to accommodate canoes or smaller boats. Most frequently these are car top carries and users should check carefully before attempting trailer discharge of a boat. Developed boat accesses are designed for trailer boat launching.

Acres - Area of the pond as determined by state sources or by estimation from U.S.G.S. maps. A dash indicates that no effective estimate could be made. Acreage is rounded to the nearest whole number.

Elevation - Given in feet above sea level as determined from U.S.G.S. maps.

Maximum and Average Depth - Determined by surveys conducted by the New Hampshire Fish and Game Department and a variety of research surveys. A dash indicates that the information was not available.

Camping - Refers to designated camping areas, either state or private, located at the pond. A blank space signifies that there are no camping facilities available, although in many cases camping facilities may be found within a short driving distance.

Comments - Refer to a variety of significant features regarding recreational use. The code numbers given in the charts refer to a list of comments found immediately after the last map in the atlas section (See Page 116.) A small black square in this column indicates that a detailed chart of the lake is provided in the depth chart section of the book.

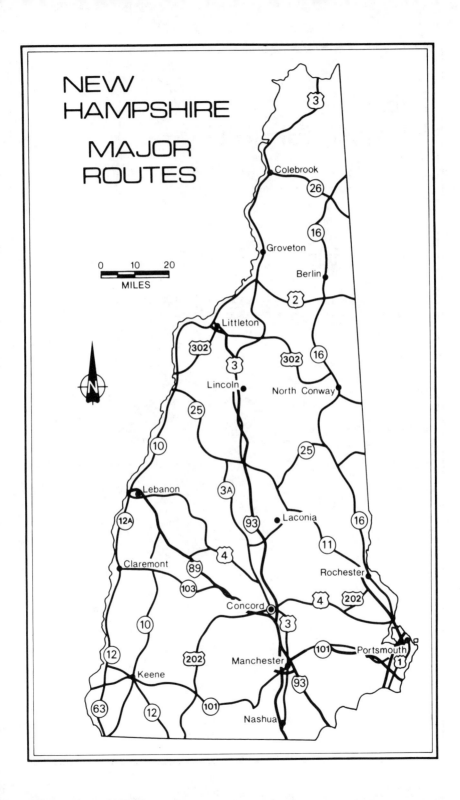

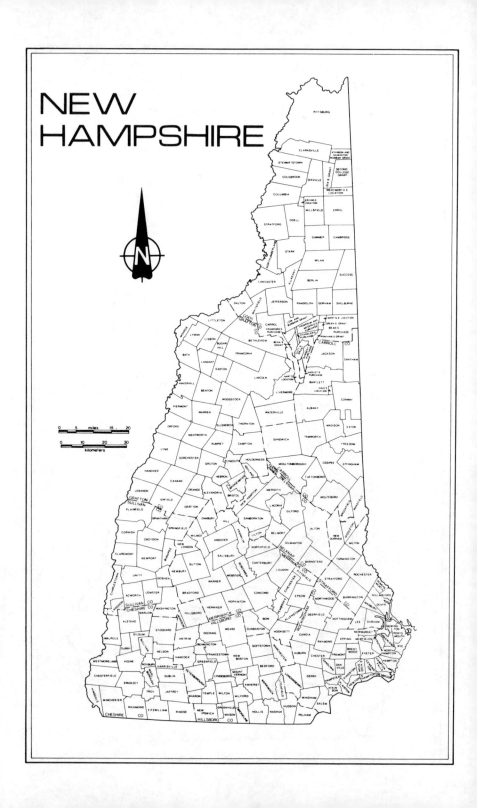

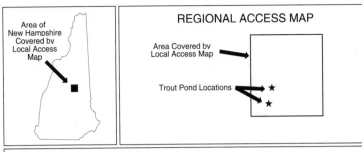

REGIONAL ACCESS MAP

LOCAL ACCESS MAP

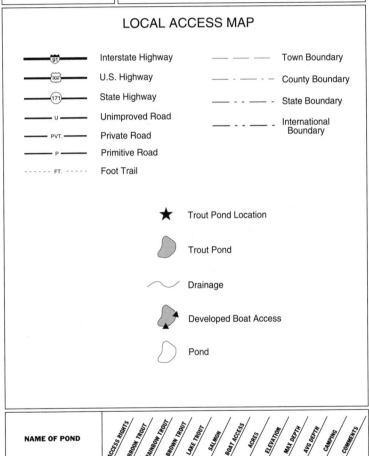

Interstate Highway (91)	Interstate Highway		— — —	Town Boundary
(302)	U.S. Highway		— · — · —	County Boundary
(171)	State Highway		— · · — ·	State Boundary
— U —	Unimproved Road		— · · — ·	International Boundary
— PVT. —	Private Road			
— P —	Primitive Road			
· · · · FT. · · · ·	Foot Trail			

★ Trout Pond Location

Trout Pond

Drainage

Developed Boat Access

Pond

NAME OF POND	ACCESS RIGHTS	BROOK TROUT	RAINBOW TROUT	BROWN TROUT	LAKE TROUT	SALMON	BOAT ACCESS	ACRES	ELEVATION	MAX. DEPTH	AVG. DEPTH	CAMPING	COMMENTS
Trout Pond	P	●	●	●	●	●	DEV	136	1043	43	21	▲	2,27 ■

CHART KEY

ACCESS RIGHTS	S - State, P- Private, F- Federal, M- Municipal C- Commercial
FISH SPECIES	Presence of Indicated Species
BOAT ACCESS	DEV- Developed UND- Undeveloped

ELEVATION
MAX. DEPTH
AVG. DEPTH
} All in Feet

CAMPING- ▲ Camping Available
COMMENTS (See Page)
- Information not Available
■ - Depth Chart Provided

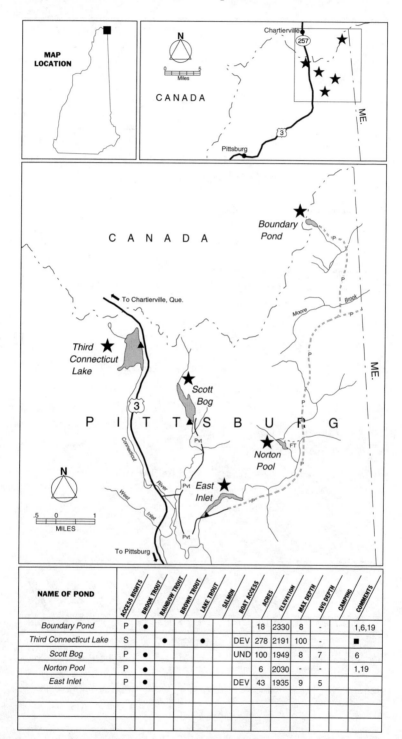

NAME OF POND	ACCESS RIGHTS	BROOK TROUT	RAINBOW TROUT	BROWN TROUT	LAKE TROUT	SALMON	BOAT ACCESS	ACRES	ELEVATION	MAX DEPTH	AVG DEPTH	CAMPING	COMMENTS
Boundary Pond	P	●						18	2330	8	-		1,6,19
Third Connecticut Lake	S		●		●		DEV	278	2191	100	-	■	
Scott Bog	P	●					UND	100	1949	8	7		6
Norton Pool	P	●						6	2030	-	-		1,19
East Inlet	P	●					DEV	43	1935	9	5		

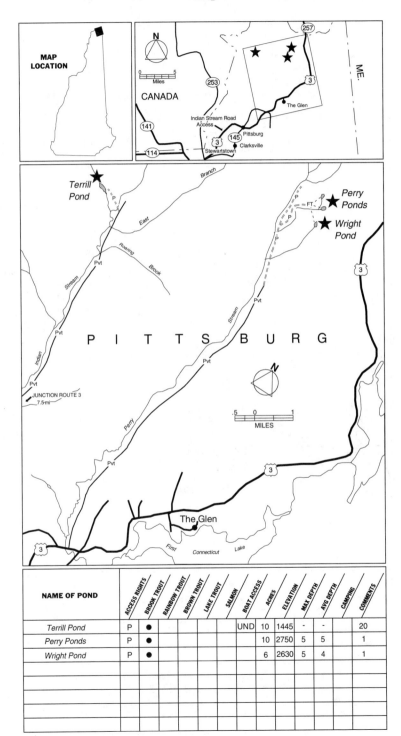

NAME OF POND	ACCESS RIGHTS	BROOK TROUT	RAINBOW TROUT	BROWN TROUT	LAKE TROUT	SALMON	BOAT ACCESS	ACRES	ELEVATION	MAX DEPTH	AVG DEPTH	CAMPING	COMMENTS
Terrill Pond	P	●					UND	10	1445	-	-		20
Perry Ponds	P	●						10	2750	5	5		1
Wright Pond	P	●						6	2630	5	4		1

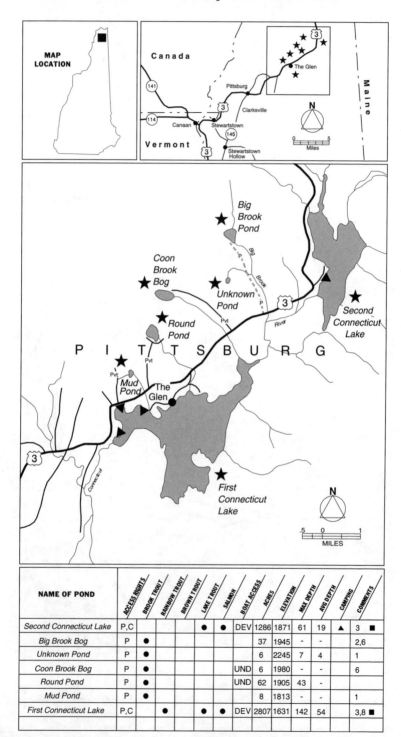

NAME OF POND	ACCESS RIGHTS	BROOK TROUT	RAINBOW TROUT	BROWN TROUT	LAKE TROUT	SALMON	BOAT ACCESS	ACRES	ELEVATION	MAX DEPTH	AVG DEPTH	CAMPING	COMMENTS
Second Connecticut Lake	P,C				●	●	DEV	1286	1871	61	19	▲	3 ■
Big Brook Bog	P	●						37	1945	-	-		2,6
Unknown Pond	P	●						6	2245	7	4		1
Coon Brook Bog	P	●					UND	6	1980	-	-		6
Round Pond	P	●					UND	62	1905	43	-		
Mud Pond	P	●						8	1813	-	-		1
First Connecticut Lake	P,C		●		●	●	DEV	2807	1631	142	54		3,8 ■

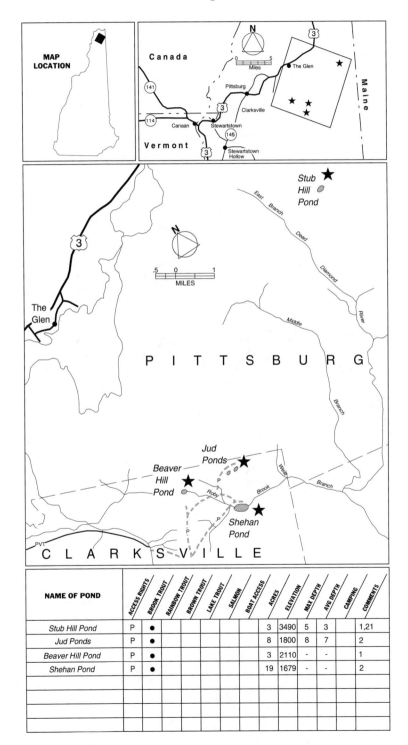

NAME OF POND	ACCESS RIGHTS	BROOK TROUT	RAINBOW TROUT	BROWN TROUT	LAKE TROUT	SALMON	BOAT ACCESS	ACRES	ELEVATION	MAX DEPTH	AVG DEPTH	CAMPING	COMMENTS
Stub Hill Pond	P	●						3	3490	5	3		1,21
Jud Ponds	P	●						8	1800	8	7		2
Beaver Hill Pond	P	●						3	2110	-	-		1
Shehan Pond	P	●						19	1679	-	-		2

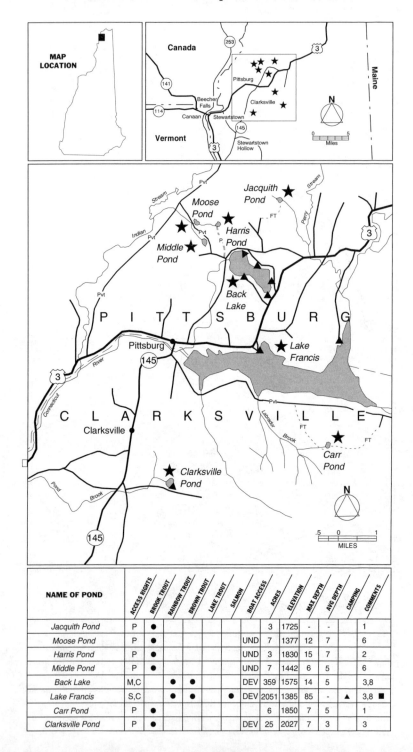

NAME OF POND	ACCESS RIGHTS	BROOK TROUT	RAINBOW TROUT	BROWN TROUT	LAKE TROUT	SALMON	BOAT ACCESS	ACRES	ELEVATION	MAX DEPTH	AVG DEPTH	CAMPING	COMMENTS
Jacquith Pond	P	●						3	1725	-	-		1
Moose Pond	P	●					UND	7	1377	12	7		6
Harris Pond	P	●					UND	3	1830	15	7		2
Middle Pond	P	●					UND	7	1442	6	5		6
Back Lake	M,C		●	●			DEV	359	1575	14	5		3,8
Lake Francis	S,C		●	●		●	DEV	2051	1385	85	-	▲	3,8 ■
Carr Pond	P	●						6	1850	7	5		1
Clarksville Pond	P	●					DEV	25	2027	7	3		3

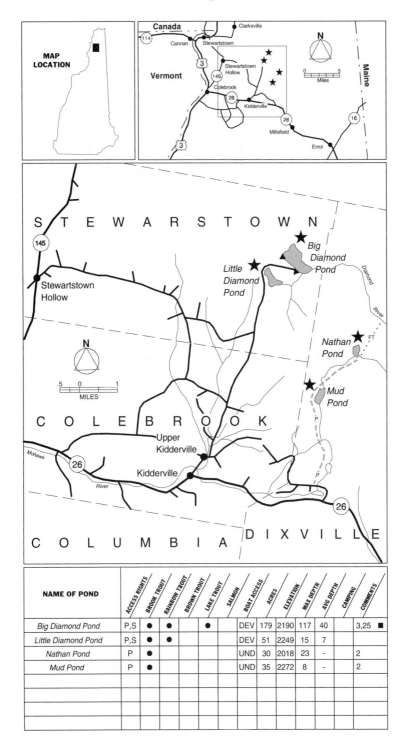

NAME OF POND	ACCESS RIGHTS	BROOK TROUT	RAINBOW TROUT	BROWN TROUT	LAKE TROUT	SALMON	BOAT ACCESS	ACRES	ELEVATION	MAX DEPTH	AVG DEPTH	CAMPING	COMMENTS
Big Diamond Pond	P,S	●	●		●		DEV	179	2190	117	40		3,25 ■
Little Diamond Pond	P,S	●	●				DEV	51	2249	15	7		
Nathan Pond	P	●					UND	30	2018	23	-		2
Mud Pond	P	●					UND	35	2272	8	-		2

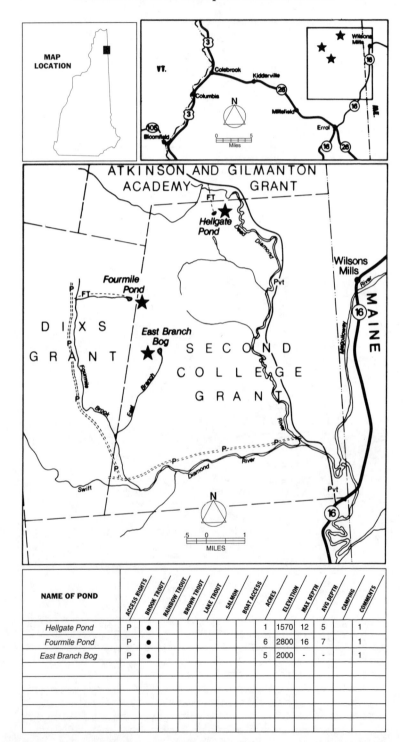

NAME OF POND	ACCESS RIGHTS	BROOK TROUT	RAINBOW TROUT	BROWN TROUT	LAKE TROUT	SALMON	BOAT ACCESS	ACRES	ELEVATION	MAX DEPTH	AVG DEPTH	CAMPING	COMMENTS
Hellgate Pond	P	●						1	1570	12	5		1
Fourmile Pond	P	●						6	2800	16	7		1
East Branch Bog	P	●						5	2000	-	-		1

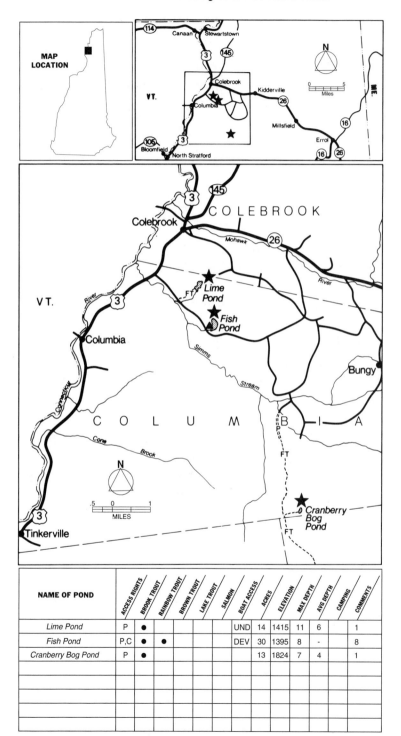

NAME OF POND	ACCESS RIGHTS	BROOK TROUT	RAINBOW TROUT	BROWN TROUT	LAKE TROUT	SALMON	BOAT ACCESS	ACRES	ELEVATION	MAX DEPTH	AVG DEPTH	CAMPING	COMMENTS
Lime Pond	P	●					UND	14	1415	11	6		1
Fish Pond	P,C	●	●				DEV	30	1395	8	-		8
Cranberry Bog Pond	P	●						13	1824	7	4		1

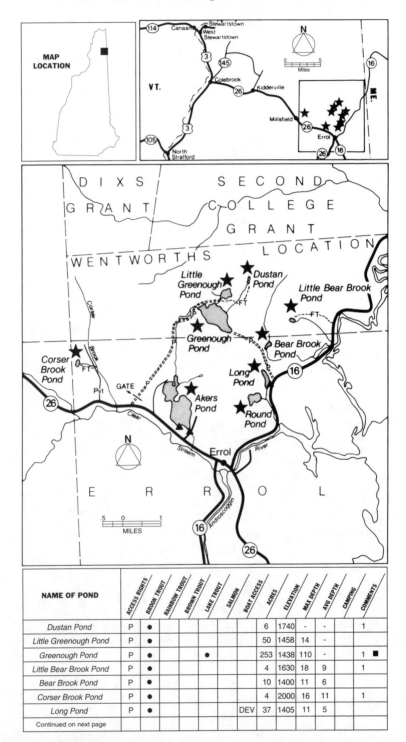

NAME OF POND	ACCESS RIGHTS	BROOK TROUT	RAINBOW TROUT	BROWN TROUT	LAKE TROUT	SALMON	BOAT ACCESS	ACRES	ELEVATION	MAX DEPTH	AVG DEPTH	CAMPING	COMMENTS
Dustan Pond	P	●						6	1740	-	-		1
Little Greenough Pond	P	●						50	1458	14	-		
Greenough Pond	P	●			●			253	1438	110	-		1 ■
Little Bear Brook Pond	P	●						4	1630	18	9		1
Bear Brook Pond	P	●						10	1400	11	6		
Corser Brook Pond	P	●						4	2000	16	11		1
Long Pond	P	●					DEV	37	1405	11	5		
Continued on next page													

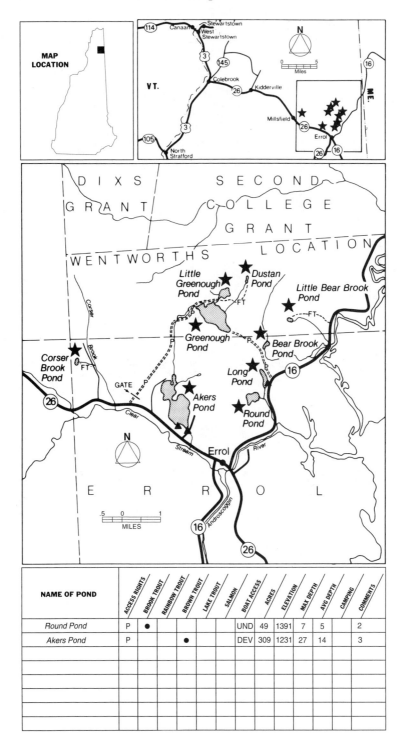

NAME OF POND	ACCESS RIGHTS	BROOK TROUT	RAINBOW TROUT	BROWN TROUT	LAKE TROUT	SALMON	BOAT ACCESS	ACRES	ELEVATION	MAX DEPTH	AVG DEPTH	CAMPING	COMMENTS
Round Pond	P	●					UND	49	1391	7	5		2
Akers Pond	P			●			DEV	309	1231	27	14		3

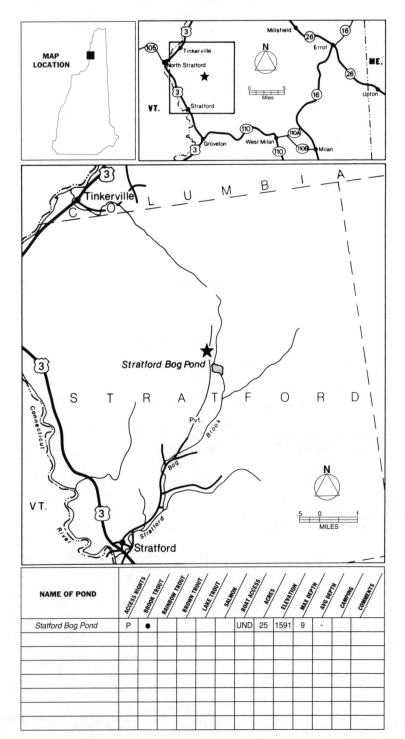

NAME OF POND	ACCESS RIGHTS	BROOK TROUT	RAINBOW TROUT	BROWN TROUT	LAKE TROUT	SALMON	BOAT ACCESS	ACRES	ELEVATION	MAX DEPTH	AVG DEPTH	CAMPING	COMMENTS
Statford Bog Pond	P	●					UND	25	1591	9	-		

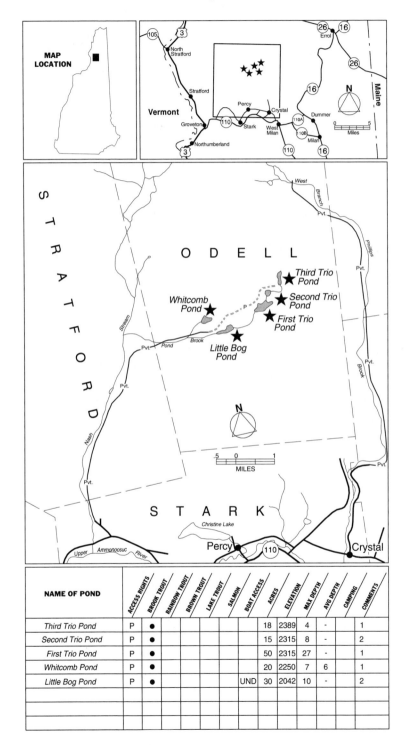

NAME OF POND	ACCESS RIGHTS	BROOK TROUT	RAINBOW TROUT	BROWN TROUT	LAKE TROUT	SALMON	BOAT ACCESS	ACRES	ELEVATION	MAX DEPTH	AVG DEPTH	CAMPING	COMMENTS
Third Trio Pond	P	●						18	2389	4	-		1
Second Trio Pond	P	●						15	2315	8	-		2
First Trio Pond	P	●						50	2315	27	-		1
Whitcomb Pond	P	●						20	2250	7	6		1
Little Bog Pond	P	●					UND	30	2042	10	-		2

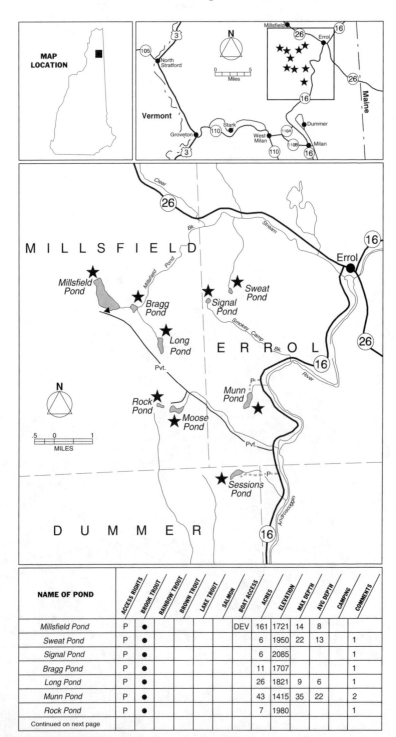

NAME OF POND	ACCESS RIGHTS	BROOK TROUT	RAINBOW TROUT	BROWN TROUT	LAKE TROUT	SALMON	BOAT ACCESS	ACRES	ELEVATION	MAX DEPTH	AVG DEPTH	CAMPING	COMMENTS
Millsfield Pond	P	●					DEV	161	1721	14	8		
Sweat Pond	P	●						6	1950	22	13		1
Signal Pond	P	●						6	2085				1
Bragg Pond	P	●						11	1707				1
Long Pond	P	●						26	1821	9	6		1
Munn Pond	P	●						43	1415	35	22		2
Rock Pond	P	●						7	1980				1
Continued on next page													

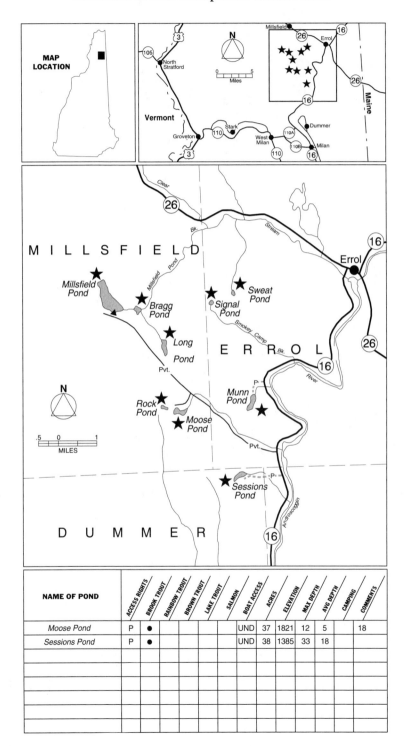

NAME OF POND	ACCESS RIGHTS	BROOK TROUT	RAINBOW TROUT	BROWN TROUT	LAKE TROUT	SALMON	BOAT ACCESS	ACRES	ELEVATION	MAX DEPTH	AVG DEPTH	CAMPING	COMMENTS
Moose Pond	P	●					UND	37	1821	12	5		18
Sessions Pond	P	●					UND	38	1385	33	18		

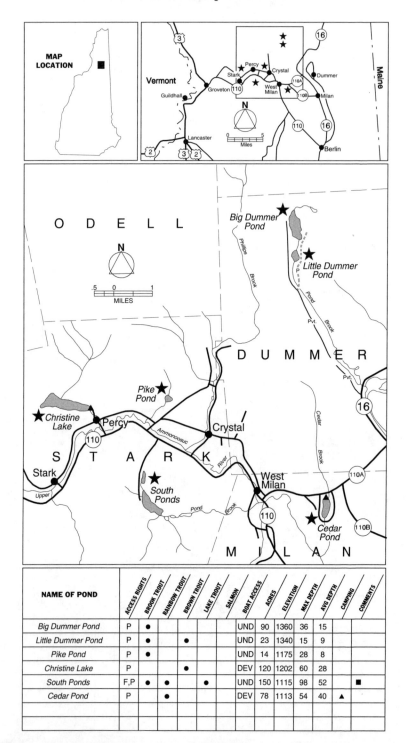

NAME OF POND	ACCESS RIGHTS	BROOK TROUT	RAINBOW TROUT	BROWN TROUT	LAKE TROUT	SALMON	BOAT ACCESS	ACRES	ELEVATION	MAX DEPTH	AVG DEPTH	CAMPING	COMMENTS
Big Dummer Pond	P	●					UND	90	1360	36	15		
Little Dummer Pond	P	●		●			UND	23	1340	15	9		
Pike Pond	P	●					UND	14	1175	28	8		
Christine Lake	P			●			DEV	120	1202	60	28		
South Ponds	F,P	●	●	●		●	UND	150	1115	98	52		■
Cedar Pond	P		●				DEV	78	1113	54	40	▲	

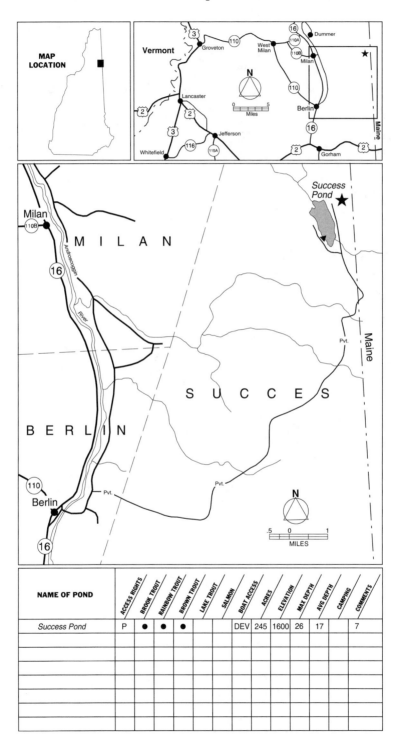

NAME OF POND	ACCESS RIGHTS	BROOK TROUT	RAINBOW TROUT	BROWN TROUT	LAKE TROUT	SALMON	BOAT ACCESS	ACRES	ELEVATION	MAX DEPTH	AVG DEPTH	CAMPING	COMMENTS
Success Pond	P	●	●	●			DEV	245	1600	26	17		7

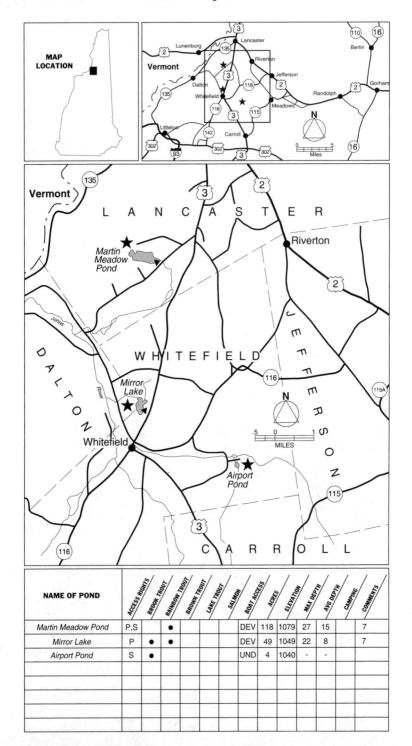

NAME OF POND	ACCESS RIGHTS	BROOK TROUT	RAINBOW TROUT	BROWN TROUT	LAKE TROUT	SALMON	BOAT ACCESS	ACRES	ELEVATION	MAX DEPTH	AVG DEPTH	CAMPING	COMMENTS
Martin Meadow Pond	P,S		●				DEV	118	1079	27	15		7
Mirror Lake	P	●	●				DEV	49	1049	22	8		7
Airport Pond	S	●					UND	4	1040	-	-		

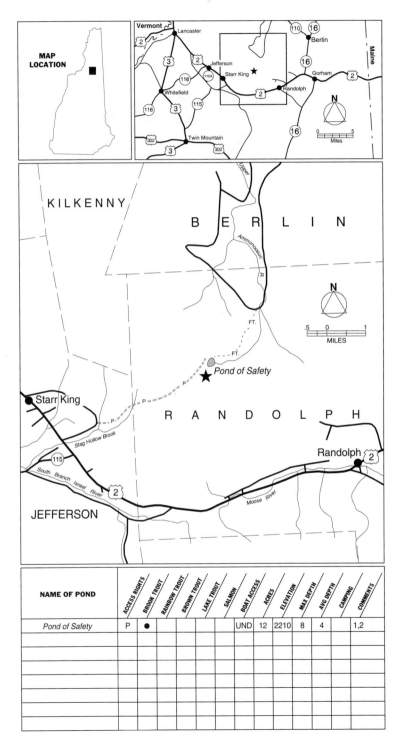

NAME OF POND	ACCESS RIGHTS	BROOK TROUT	RAINBOW TROUT	BROWN TROUT	LAKE TROUT	SALMON	BOAT ACCESS	ACRES	ELEVATION	MAX DEPTH	AVG DEPTH	CAMPING	COMMENTS
Pond of Safety	P	●					UND	12	2210	8	4		1,2

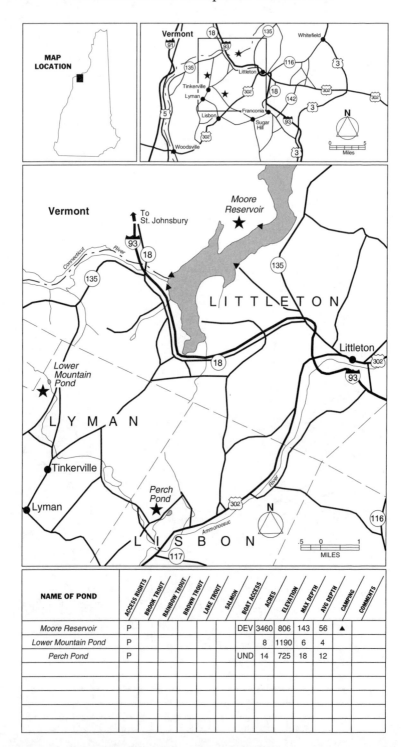

NAME OF POND	ACCESS RIGHTS	BROOK TROUT	RAINBOW TROUT	BROWN TROUT	LAKE TROUT	SALMON	BOAT ACCESS	ACRES	ELEVATION	MAX DEPTH	AVG DEPTH	CAMPING	COMMENTS
Moore Reservoir	P						DEV	3460	806	143	56	▲	
Lower Mountain Pond	P							8	1190	6	4		
Perch Pond	P						UND	14	725	18	12		

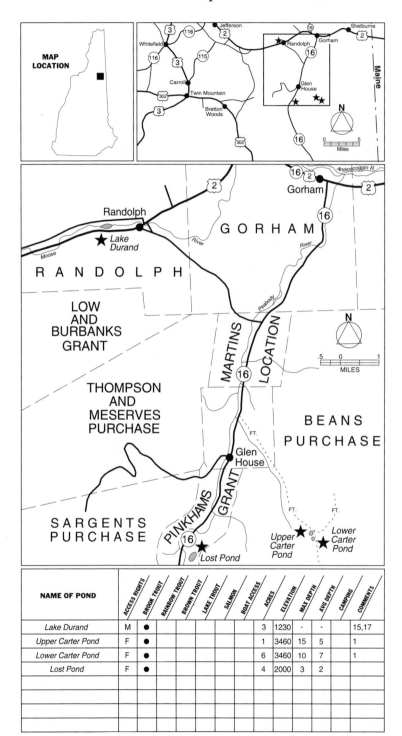

NAME OF POND	ACCESS RIGHTS	BROOK TROUT	RAINBOW TROUT	BROWN TROUT	LAKE TROUT	SALMON	BOAT ACCESS	ACRES	ELEVATION	MAX DEPTH	AVG DEPTH	CAMPING	COMMENTS
Lake Durand	M	●						3	1230	-	-		15,17
Upper Carter Pond	F	●						1	3460	15	5		1
Lower Carter Pond	F	●						6	3460	10	7		1
Lost Pond	F	●						4	2000	3	2		

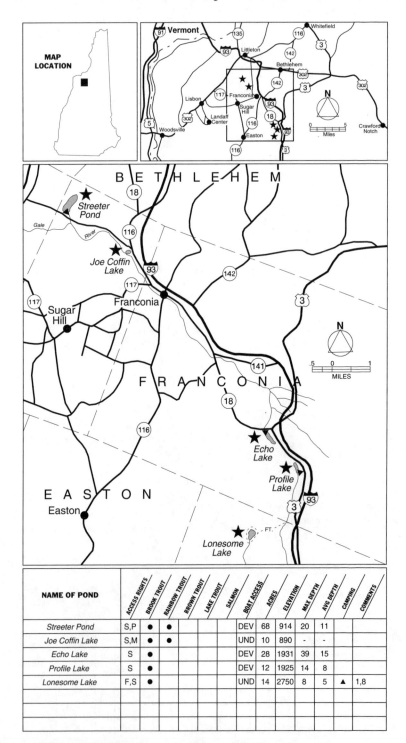

NAME OF POND	ACCESS RIGHTS	BROOK TROUT	RAINBOW TROUT	BROWN TROUT	LAKE TROUT	SALMON	BOAT ACCESS	ACRES	ELEVATION	MAX DEPTH	AVG DEPTH	CAMPING	COMMENTS
Streeter Pond	S,P	●	●				DEV	68	914	20	11		
Joe Coffin Lake	S,M	●	●				UND	10	890	-	-		
Echo Lake	S	●					DEV	28	1931	39	15		
Profile Lake	S	●					DEV	12	1925	14	8		
Lonesome Lake	F,S	●					UND	14	2750	8	5	▲	1,8

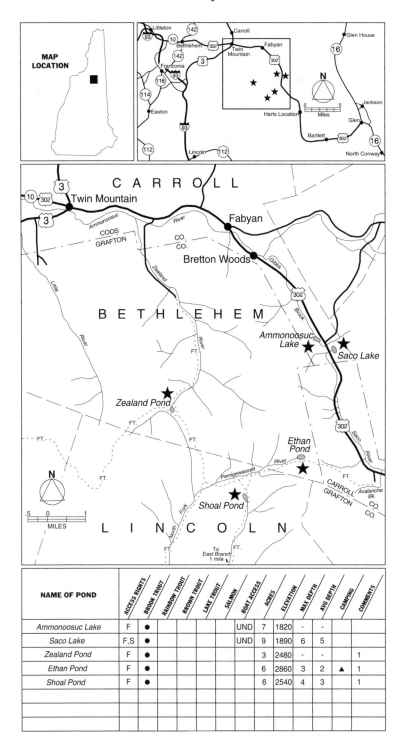

NAME OF POND	ACCESS RIGHTS	BROOK TROUT	RAINBOW TROUT	BROWN TROUT	LAKE TROUT	SALMON	BOAT ACCESS	ACRES	ELEVATION	MAX DEPTH	AVG DEPTH	CAMPING	COMMENTS
Ammonoosuc Lake	F	●					UND	7	1820	-	-		
Saco Lake	F,S	●					UND	9	1890	6	5		
Zealand Pond	F	●						3	2480	-	-		1
Ethan Pond	F	●						6	2860	3	2	▲	1
Shoal Pond	F	●						6	2540	4	3		1

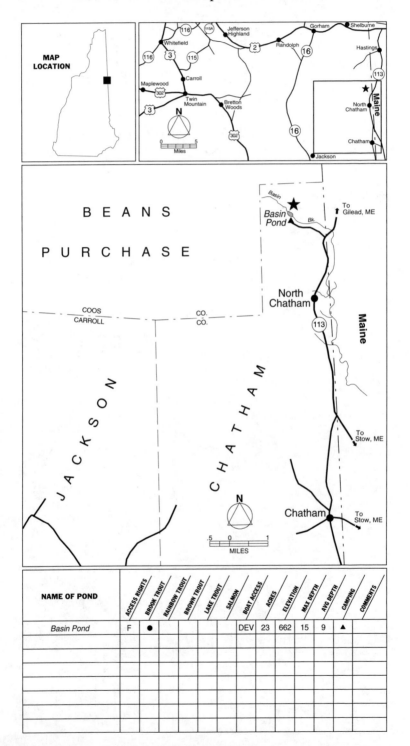

NAME OF POND	ACCESS RIGHTS	BROOK TROUT	RAINBOW TROUT	BROWN TROUT	LAKE TROUT	SALMON	BOAT ACCESS	ACRES	ELEVATION	MAX DEPTH	AVG DEPTH	CAMPING	COMMENTS
Basin Pond	F	●					DEV	23	662	15	9	▲	

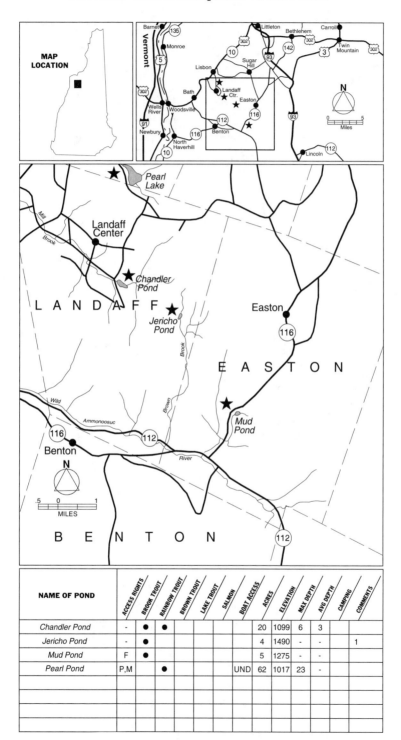

NAME OF POND	ACCESS RIGHTS	BROOK TROUT	RAINBOW TROUT	BROWN TROUT	LAKE TROUT	SALMON	BOAT ACCESS	ACRES	ELEVATION	MAX DEPTH	AVG DEPTH	CAMPING	COMMENTS
Chandler Pond	-	●	●					20	1099	6	3		
Jericho Pond	-	●						4	1490	-	-		1
Mud Pond	F	●						5	1275	-	-		
Pearl Pond	P,M		●				UND	62	1017	23	-		

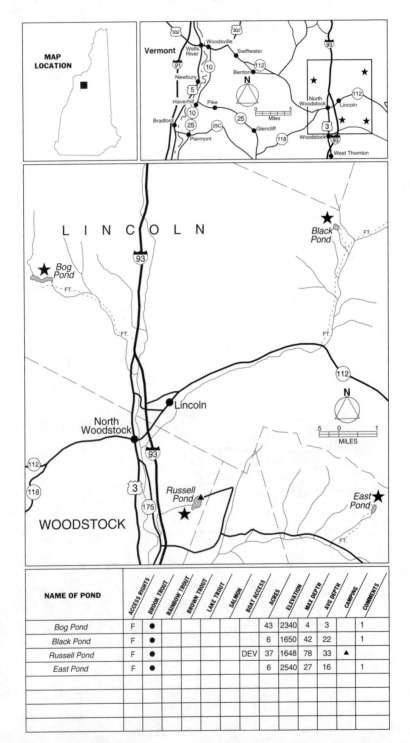

NAME OF POND	ACCESS RIGHTS	BROOK TROUT	RAINBOW TROUT	BROWN TROUT	LAKE TROUT	SALMON	BOAT ACCESS	ACRES	ELEVATION	MAX DEPTH	AVG DEPTH	CAMPING	COMMENTS
Bog Pond	F	●						43	2340	4	3		1
Black Pond	F	●						6	1650	42	22		1
Russell Pond	F	●					DEV	37	1648	78	33	▲	
East Pond	F	●						6	2540	27	16		1

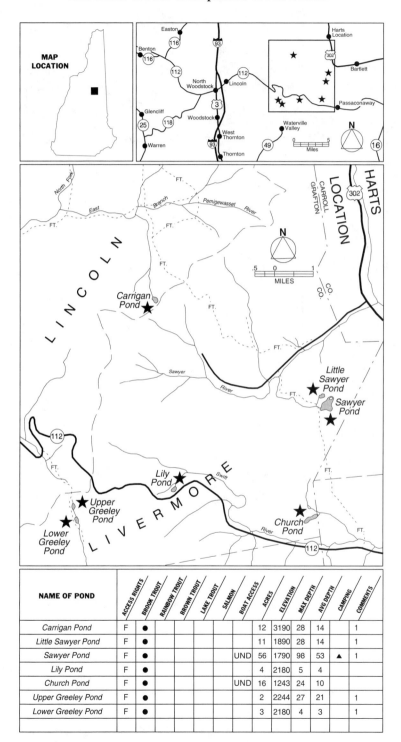

NAME OF POND	ACCESS RIGHTS	BROOK TROUT	RAINBOW TROUT	BROWN TROUT	LAKE TROUT	SALMON	BOAT ACCESS	ACRES	ELEVATION	MAX DEPTH	AVG DEPTH	CAMPING	COMMENTS
Carrigan Pond	F	●						12	3190	28	14		1
Little Sawyer Pond	F	●						11	1890	28	14		1
Sawyer Pond	F	●					UND	56	1790	98	53	▲	1
Lily Pond	F	●						4	2180	5	4		
Church Pond	F	●					UND	16	1243	24	10		
Upper Greeley Pond	F	●						2	2244	27	21		1
Lower Greeley Pond	F	●						3	2180	4	3		1

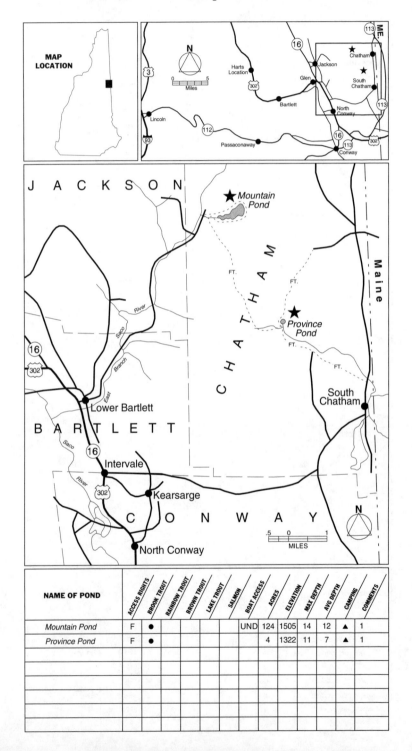

NAME OF POND	ACCESS RIGHTS	BROOK TROUT	RAINBOW TROUT	BROWN TROUT	LAKE TROUT	SALMON	BOAT ACCESS	ACRES	ELEVATION	MAX DEPTH	AVG DEPTH	CAMPING	COMMENTS
Mountain Pond	F	●					UND	124	1505	14	12	▲	1
Province Pond	F	●						4	1322	11	7	▲	1

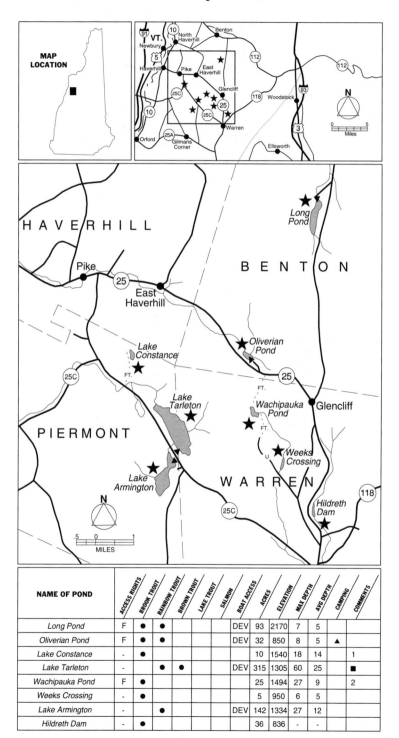

NAME OF POND	ACCESS RIGHTS	BROOK TROUT	RAINBOW TROUT	BROWN TROUT	LAKE TROUT	SALMON	BOAT ACCESS	ACRES	ELEVATION	MAX DEPTH	AVG DEPTH	CAMPING	COMMENTS
Long Pond	F	●	●				DEV	93	2170	7	5		
Oliverian Pond	F	●	●				DEV	32	850	8	5	▲	
Lake Constance	-	●						10	1540	18	14		1
Lake Tarleton	-		●	●			DEV	315	1305	60	25		■
Wachipauka Pond	F	●						25	1494	27	9		2
Weeks Crossing	-	●						5	950	6	5		
Lake Armington	-		●				DEV	142	1334	27	12		
Hildreth Dam	-	●						36	836	-	-		

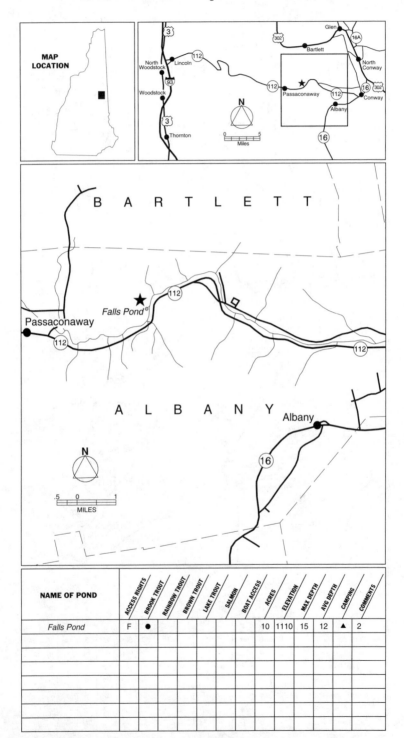

NAME OF POND	ACCESS RIGHTS	BROOK TROUT	RAINBOW TROUT	BROWN TROUT	LAKE TROUT	SALMON	BOAT ACCESS	ACRES	ELEVATION	MAX DEPTH	AVG DEPTH	CAMPING	COMMENTS
Falls Pond	F	●						10	1110	15	12	▲	2

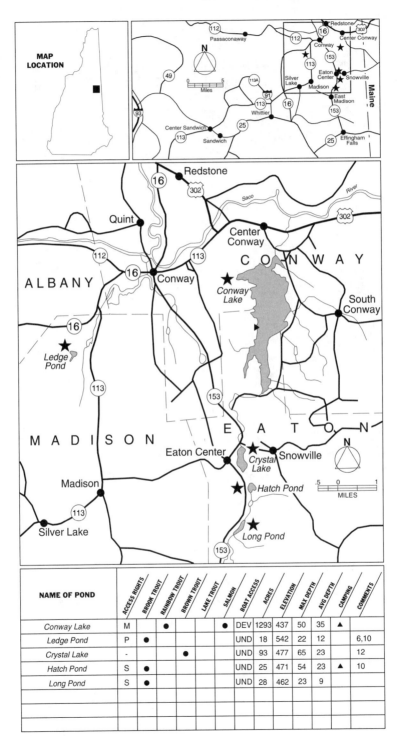

NAME OF POND	ACCESS RIGHTS	BROOK TROUT	RAINBOW TROUT	BROWN TROUT	LAKE TROUT	SALMON	BOAT ACCESS	ACRES	ELEVATION	MAX DEPTH	AVG DEPTH	CAMPING	COMMENTS
Conway Lake	M		●			●	DEV	1293	437	50	35	▲	
Ledge Pond	P	●					UND	18	542	22	12		6,10
Crystal Lake	-			●			UND	93	477	65	23		12
Hatch Pond	S	●					UND	25	471	54	23	▲	10
Long Pond	S	●					UND	28	462	23	9		

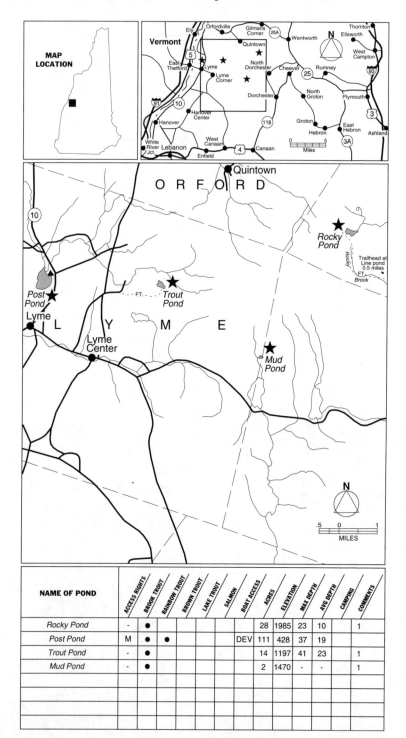

NAME OF POND	ACCESS RIGHTS	BROOK TROUT	RAINBOW TROUT	BROWN TROUT	LAKE TROUT	SALMON	BOAT ACCESS	ACRES	ELEVATION	MAX DEPTH	AVG DEPTH	CAMPING	COMMENTS
Rocky Pond	-	●						28	1985	23	10		1
Post Pond	M	●	●				DEV	111	428	37	19		
Trout Pond	-	●						14	1197	41	23		1
Mud Pond	-	●						2	1470	-	-		1

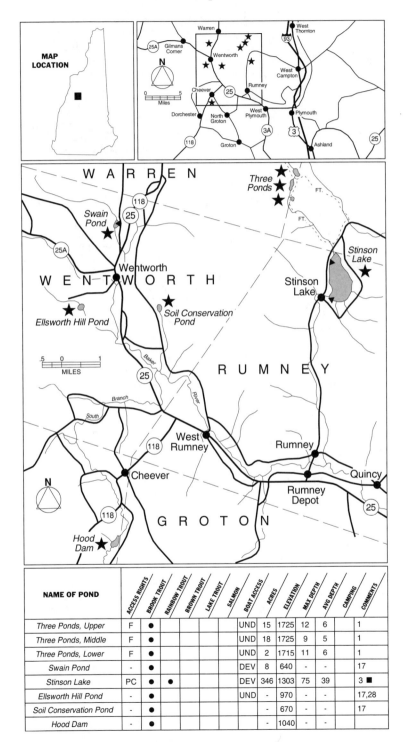

NAME OF POND	ACCESS RIGHTS	BROOK TROUT	RAINBOW TROUT	BROWN TROUT	LAKE TROUT	SALMON	BOAT ACCESS	ACRES	ELEVATION	MAX DEPTH	AVG DEPTH	CAMPING	COMMENTS
Three Ponds, Upper	F	●					UND	15	1725	12	6		1
Three Ponds, Middle	F	●					UND	18	1725	9	5		1
Three Ponds, Lower	F	●					UND	2	1715	11	6		1
Swain Pond	-	●					DEV	8	640	-	-		17
Stinson Lake	PC	●	●				DEV	346	1303	75	39		3 ■
Ellsworth Hill Pond	-	●					UND	-	970	-	-		17,28
Soil Conservation Pond	-	●						-	670	-	-		17
Hood Dam	-	●						-	1040	-	-		

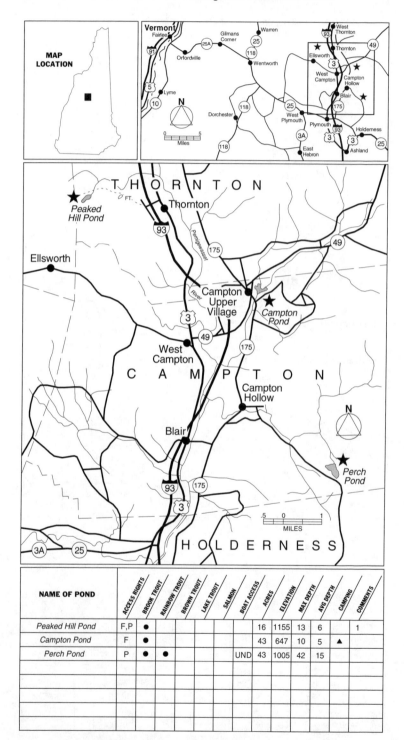

NAME OF POND	ACCESS RIGHTS	BROOK TROUT	RAINBOW TROUT	BROWN TROUT	LAKE TROUT	SALMON	BOAT ACCESS	ACRES	ELEVATION	MAX DEPTH	AVG DEPTH	CAMPING	COMMENTS
Peaked Hill Pond	F,P	●						16	1155	13	6		1
Campton Pond	F	●						43	647	10	5	▲	
Perch Pond	P	●	●				UND	43	1005	42	15		

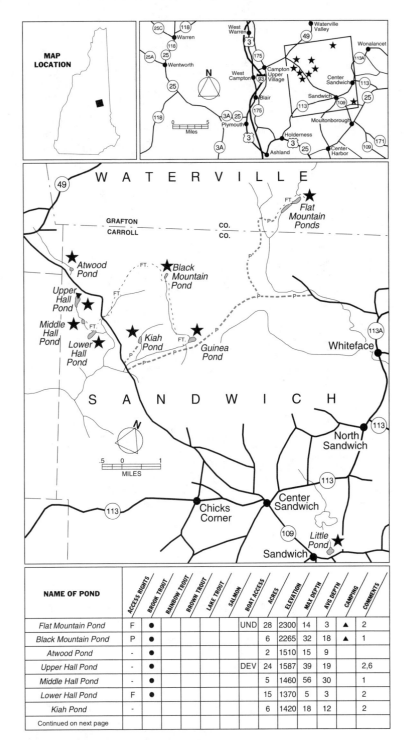

NAME OF POND	ACCESS RIGHTS	BROOK TROUT	RAINBOW TROUT	BROWN TROUT	LAKE TROUT	SALMON	BOAT ACCESS	ACRES	ELEVATION	MAX DEPTH	AVG DEPTH	CAMPING	COMMENTS
Flat Mountain Pond	F	●					UND	28	2300	14	3	▲	2
Black Mountain Pond	P	●						6	2265	32	18	▲	1
Atwood Pond	-	●						2	1510	15	9		
Upper Hall Pond	-	●					DEV	24	1587	39	19		2,6
Middle Hall Pond	-	●						5	1460	56	30		1
Lower Hall Pond	F	●						15	1370	5	3		2
Kiah Pond	-							6	1420	18	12		2
Continued on next page													

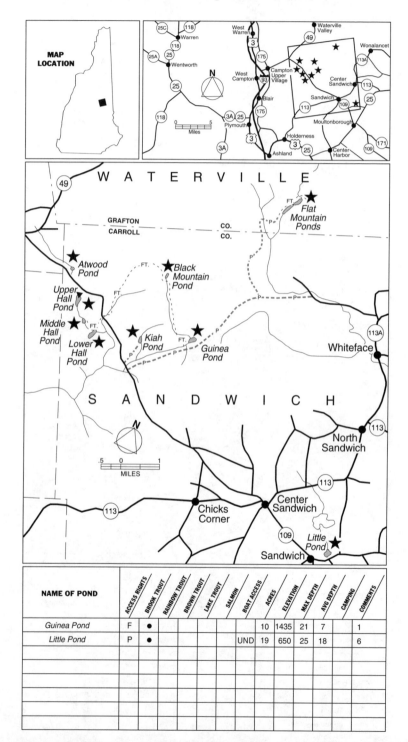

NAME OF POND	ACCESS RIGHTS	BROOK TROUT	RAINBOW TROUT	BROWN TROUT	LAKE TROUT	SALMON	BOAT ACCESS	ACRES	ELEVATION	MAX DEPTH	AVG DEPTH	CAMPING	COMMENTS
Guinea Pond	F	●						10	1435	21	7		1
Little Pond	P	●					UND	19	650	25	18		6

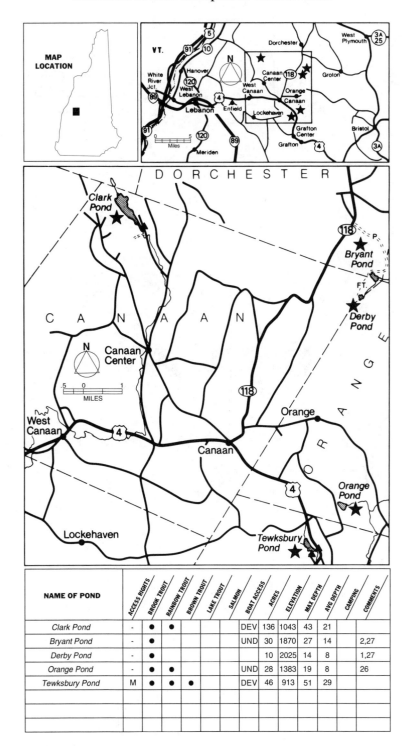

NAME OF POND	ACCESS RIGHTS	BROOK TROUT	RAINBOW TROUT	BROWN TROUT	LAKE TROUT	SALMON	BOAT ACCESS	ACRES	ELEVATION	MAX DEPTH	AVG DEPTH	CAMPING	COMMENTS
Clark Pond	-	●	●				DEV	136	1043	43	21		
Bryant Pond	-	●					UND	30	1870	27	14		2,27
Derby Pond	-	●						10	2025	14	8		1,27
Orange Pond	-	●	●				UND	28	1383	19	8		26
Tewksbury Pond	M	●	●	●			DEV	46	913	51	29		

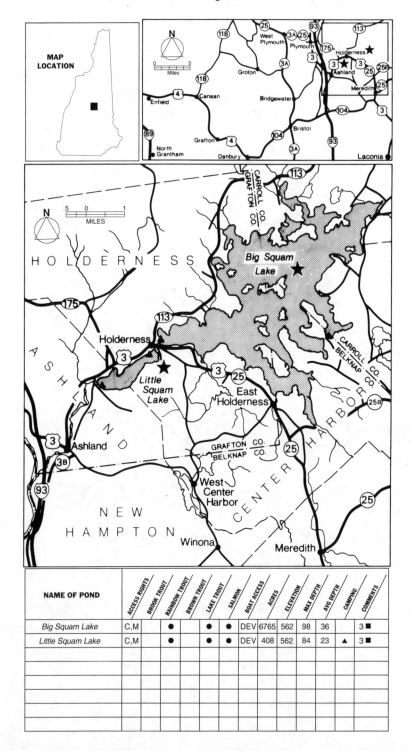

NAME OF POND	ACCESS RIGHTS	BROOK TROUT	RAINBOW TROUT	BROWN TROUT	LAKE TROUT	SALMON	BOAT ACCESS	ACRES	ELEVATION	MAX DEPTH	AVG DEPTH	CAMPING	COMMENTS
Big Squam Lake	C,M	●		●	●		DEV	6765	562	98	36		3 ■
Little Squam Lake	C,M	●		●	●		DEV	408	562	84	23	▲	3 ■

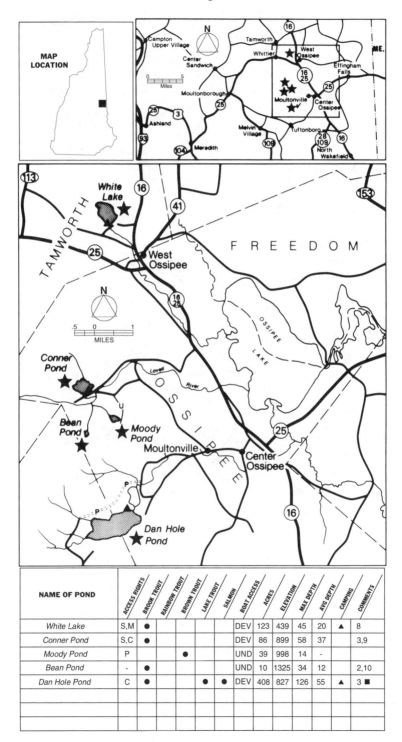

NAME OF POND	ACCESS RIGHTS	BROOK TROUT	RAINBOW TROUT	BROWN TROUT	LAKE TROUT	SALMON	BOAT ACCESS	ACRES	ELEVATION	MAX DEPTH	AVG DEPTH	CAMPING	COMMENTS
White Lake	S,M	●					DEV	123	439	45	20	▲	8
Conner Pond	S,C	●					DEV	86	899	58	37		3,9
Moody Pond	P			●			UND	39	998	14	-		
Bean Pond	-	●					UND	10	1325	34	12		2,10
Dan Hole Pond	C	●			●	●	DEV	408	827	126	55	▲	3 ■

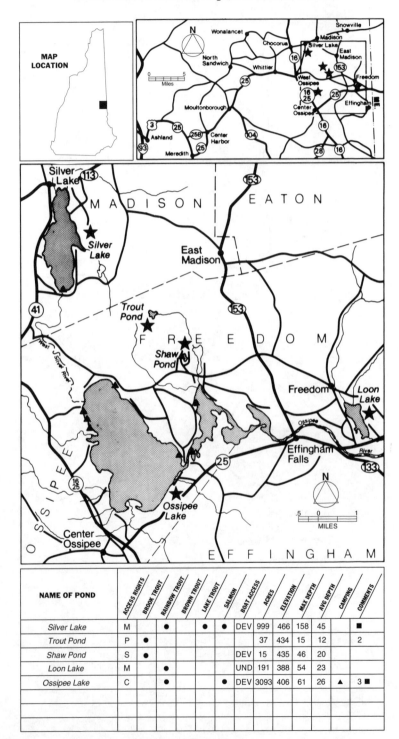

NAME OF POND	ACCESS RIGHTS	BROOK TROUT	RAINBOW TROUT	BROWN TROUT	LAKE TROUT	SALMON	BOAT ACCESS	ACRES	ELEVATION	MAX DEPTH	AVG DEPTH	CAMPING	COMMENTS
Silver Lake	M		●		●	●	DEV	999	466	158	45		■
Trout Pond	P	●						37	434	15	12		2
Shaw Pond	S	●					DEV	15	435	46	20		
Loon Lake	M		●				UND	191	388	54	23		
Ossipee Lake	C		●			●	DEV	3093	406	61	26	▲	3 ■

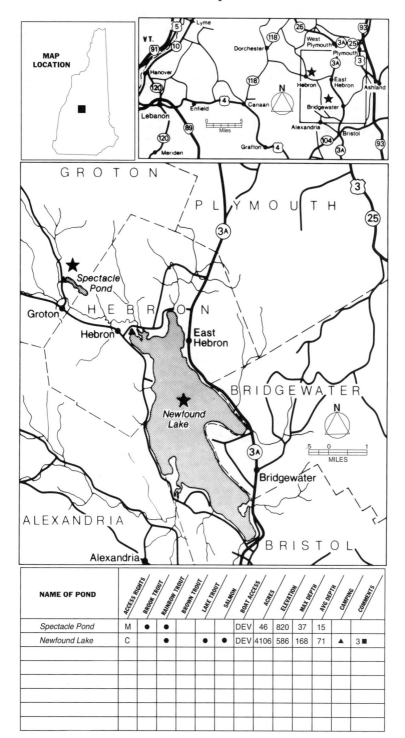

NAME OF POND	ACCESS RIGHTS	BROOK TROUT	RAINBOW TROUT	BROWN TROUT	LAKE TROUT	SALMON	BOAT ACCESS	ACRES	ELEVATION	MAX DEPTH	AVG DEPTH	CAMPING	COMMENTS
Spectacle Pond	M	●	●				DEV	46	820	37	15		
Newfound Lake	C		●		●	●	DEV	4106	586	168	71	▲	3■

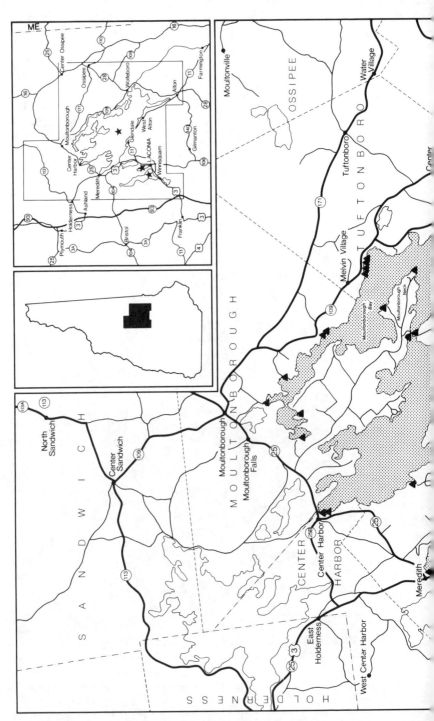

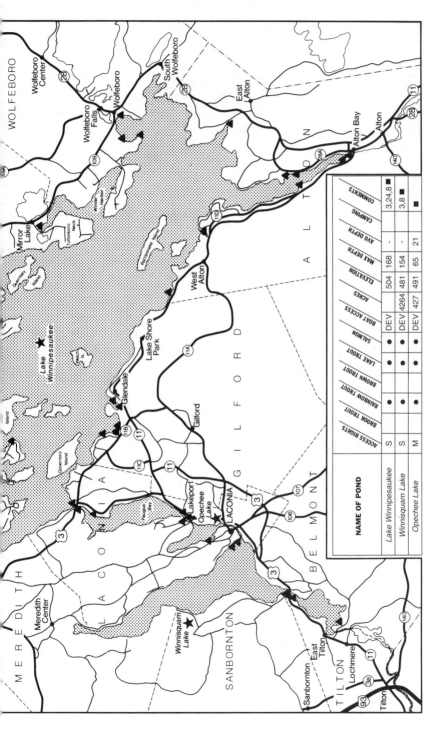

NAME OF POND	ACCESS RIGHTS	BROOK TROUT	RAINBOW TROUT	BROWN TROUT	LAKE TROUT	SALMON	BOAT ACCESS	ACRES	ELEVATION	MAX DEPTH	AVG DEPTH	CAMPING	COMMENTS
Lake Winnipesaukee	S				●	●	DEV	504	168	-			3,24,8 ■
Winnisquam Lake	S		●		●	●	DEV	4264	481	154	-		3,8 ■
Opechee Lake	M		●		●	●	DEV	427	491	65	21		■

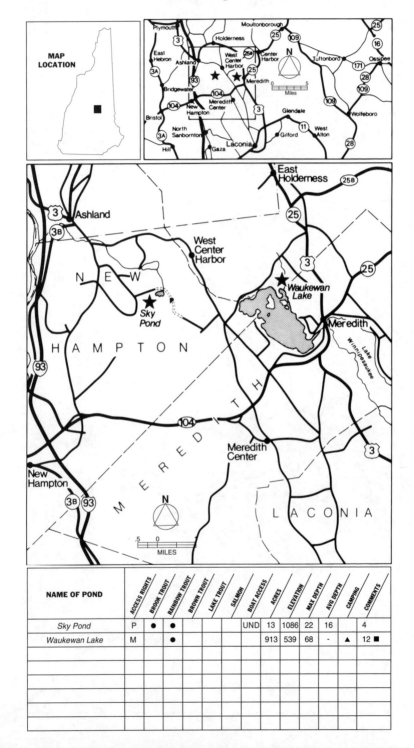

NAME OF POND	ACCESS RIGHTS	BROOK TROUT	RAINBOW TROUT	BROWN TROUT	LAKE TROUT	SALMON	BOAT ACCESS	ACRES	ELEVATION	MAX DEPTH	AVG DEPTH	CAMPING	COMMENTS
Sky Pond	P	●	●				UND	13	1086	22	16		4
Waukewan Lake	M		●					913	539	68	-	▲	12 ■

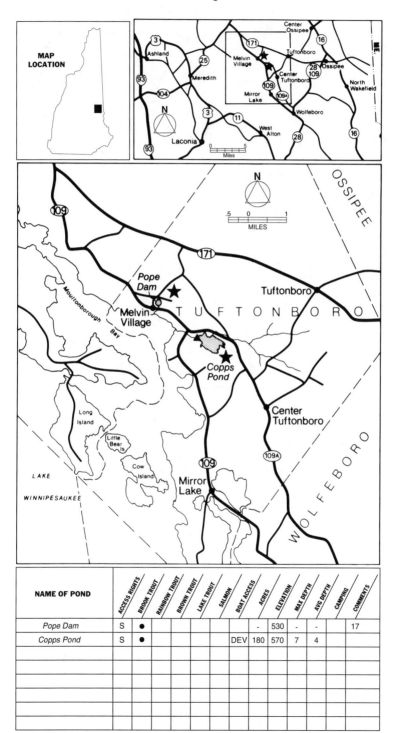

NAME OF POND	ACCESS RIGHTS	BROOK TROUT	RAINBOW TROUT	BROWN TROUT	LAKE TROUT	SALMON	BOAT ACCESS	ACRES	ELEVATION	MAX DEPTH	AVG DEPTH	CAMPING	COMMENTS
Pope Dam	S	●						-	530	-	-		17
Copps Pond	S	●					DEV	180	570	7	4		

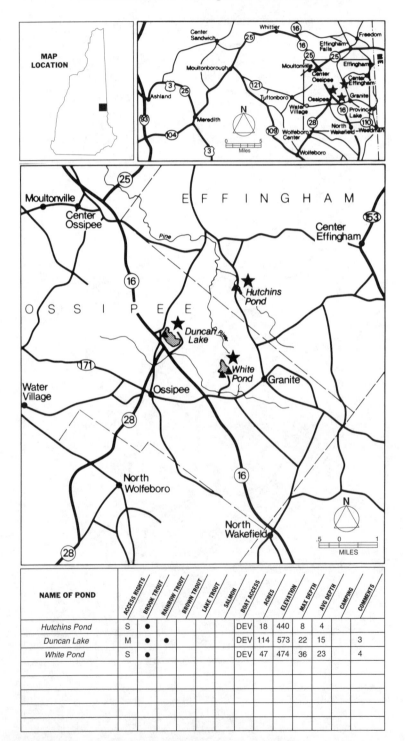

NAME OF POND	ACCESS RIGHTS	BROOK TROUT	RAINBOW TROUT	BROWN TROUT	LAKE TROUT	SALMON	BOAT ACCESS	ACRES	ELEVATION	MAX DEPTH	AVG DEPTH	CAMPING	COMMENTS
Hutchins Pond	S	●					DEV	18	440	8	4		
Duncan Lake	M	●	●				DEV	114	573	22	15		3
White Pond	S	●					DEV	47	474	36	23		4

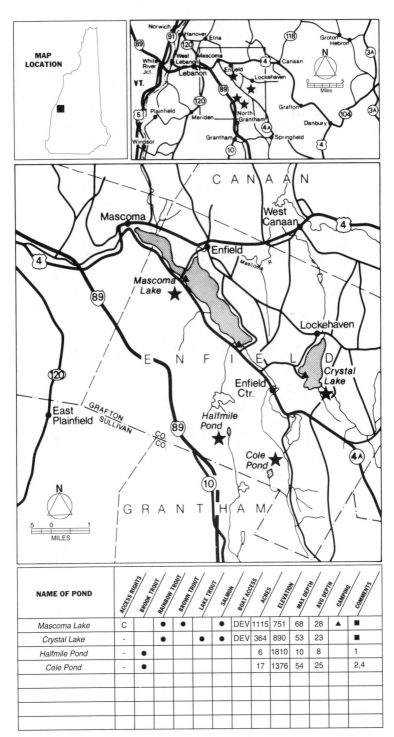

NAME OF POND	ACCESS RIGHTS	BROOK TROUT	RAINBOW TROUT	BROWN TROUT	LAKE TROUT	SALMON	BOAT ACCESS	ACRES	ELEVATION	MAX DEPTH	AVG DEPTH	CAMPING	COMMENTS
Mascoma Lake	C		●	●		●	DEV	1115	751	68	28	▲	■
Crystal Lake	-		●		●	●	DEV	364	890	53	23		■
Halfmile Pond	-	●						6	1810	10	8		1
Cole Pond	-	●						17	1376	54	25		2,4

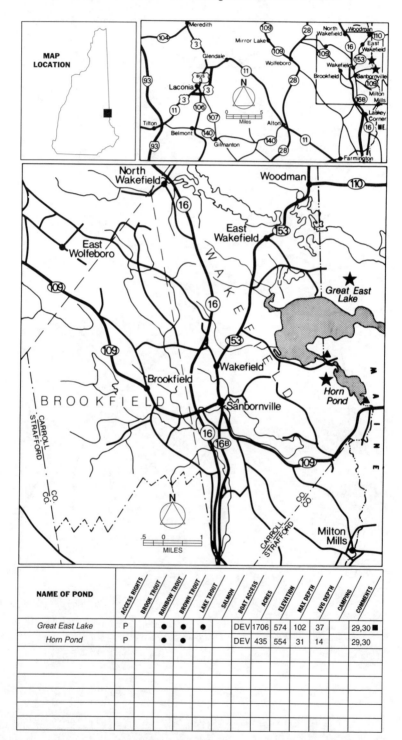

NAME OF POND	ACCESS RIGHTS	BROOK TROUT	RAINBOW TROUT	BROWN TROUT	LAKE TROUT	SALMON	BOAT ACCESS	ACRES	ELEVATION	MAX DEPTH	AVG DEPTH	CAMPING	COMMENTS
Great East Lake	P	●	●	●			DEV	1706	574	102	37		29,30 ■
Horn Pond	P	●	●				DEV	435	554	31	14		29,30

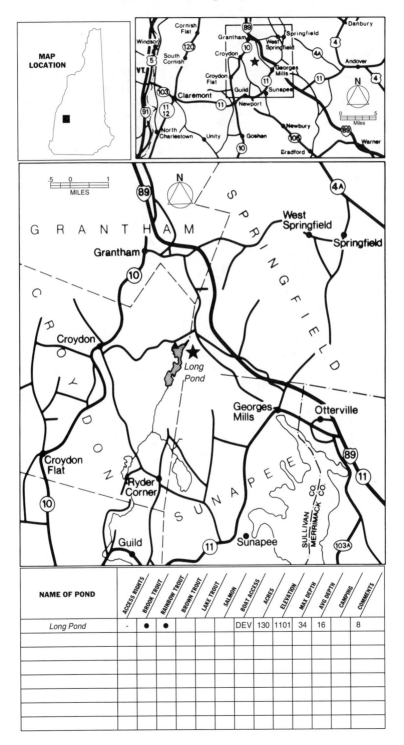

NAME OF POND	ACCESS RIGHTS	BROOK TROUT	RAINBOW TROUT	BROWN TROUT	LAKE TROUT	SALMON	BOAT ACCESS	ACRES	ELEVATION	MAX DEPTH	AVG DEPTH	CAMPING	COMMENTS
Long Pond	-	●	●				DEV	130	1101	34	16		8

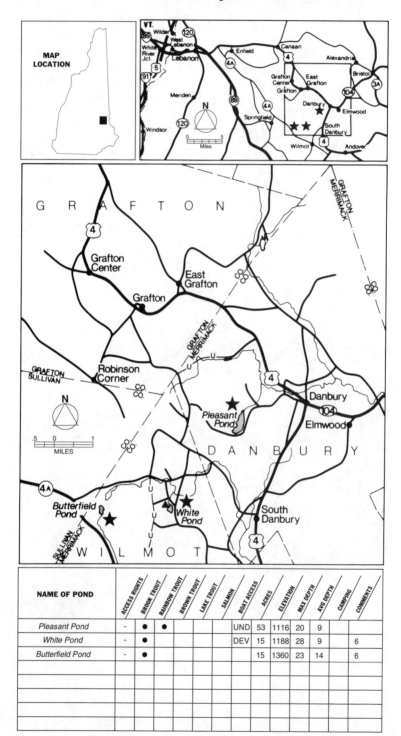

NAME OF POND	ACCESS RIGHTS	BROOK TROUT	RAINBOW TROUT	BROWN TROUT	LAKE TROUT	SALMON	BOAT ACCESS	ACRES	ELEVATION	MAX DEPTH	AVG DEPTH	CAMPING	COMMENTS
Pleasant Pond	-	●	●				UND	53	1116	20	9		
White Pond	-	●					DEV	15	1188	28	9	6	
Butterfield Pond	-	●						15	1360	23	14	6	

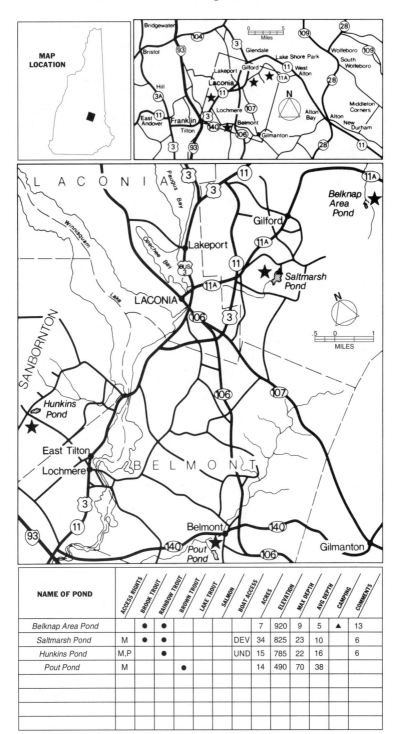

NAME OF POND	ACCESS RIGHTS	BROOK TROUT	RAINBOW TROUT	BROWN TROUT	LAKE TROUT	SALMON	BOAT ACCESS	ACRES	ELEVATION	MAX DEPTH	AVG DEPTH	CAMPING	COMMENTS
Belknap Area Pond		●	●					7	920	9	5	▲	13
Saltmarsh Pond	M	●	●				DEV	34	825	23	10		6
Hunkins Pond	M,P		●				UND	15	785	22	16		6
Pout Pond	M			●				14	490	70	38		

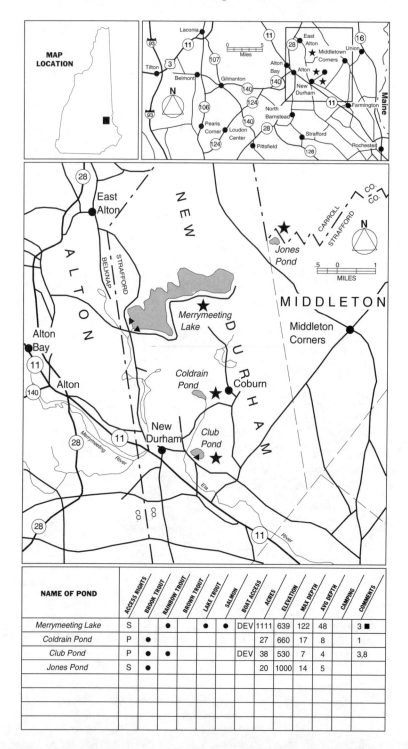

NAME OF POND	ACCESS RIGHTS	BROOK TROUT	RAINBOW TROUT	BROWN TROUT	LAKE TROUT	SALMON	BOAT ACCESS	ACRES	ELEVATION	MAX DEPTH	AVG DEPTH	CAMPING	COMMENTS
Merrymeeting Lake	S		●		●	●	DEV	1111	639	122	48		3 ■
Coldrain Pond	P	●						27	660	17	8		1
Club Pond	P	●	●				DEV	38	530	7	4		3,8
Jones Pond	S	●						20	1000	14	5		

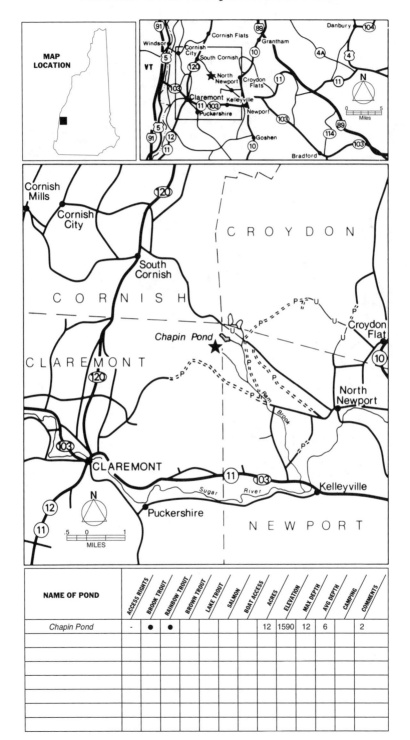

NAME OF POND	ACCESS RIGHTS	BROOK TROUT	RAINBOW TROUT	BROWN TROUT	LAKE TROUT	SALMON	BOAT ACCESS	ACRES	ELEVATION	MAX DEPTH	AVG DEPTH	CAMPING	COMMENTS
Chapin Pond	-	●	●					12	1590	12	6		2

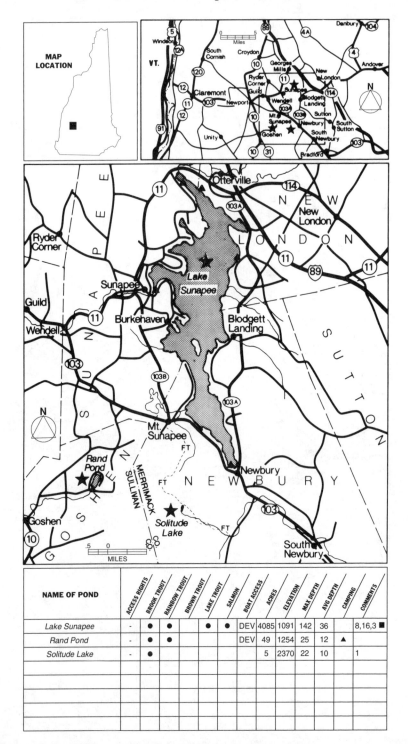

NAME OF POND	ACCESS RIGHTS	BROOK TROUT	RAINBOW TROUT	BROWN TROUT	LAKE TROUT	SALMON	BOAT ACCESS	ACRES	ELEVATION	MAX DEPTH	AVG DEPTH	CAMPING	COMMENTS
Lake Sunapee	-	●	●		●	●	DEV	4085	1091	142	36		8,16,3 ■
Rand Pond	-	●	●				DEV	49	1254	25	12	▲	
Solitude Lake	-	●						5	2370	22	10		1

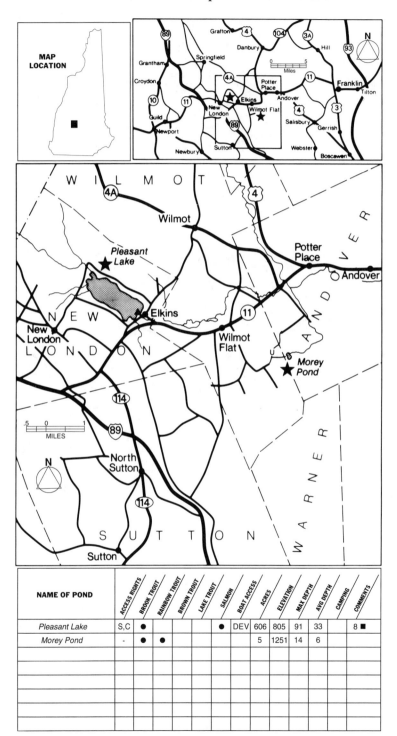

NAME OF POND	ACCESS RIGHTS	BROOK TROUT	RAINBOW TROUT	BROWN TROUT	LAKE TROUT	SALMON	BOAT ACCESS	ACRES	ELEVATION	MAX DEPTH	AVG DEPTH	CAMPING	COMMENTS
Pleasant Lake	S,C	●				●	DEV	606	805	91	33		8 ■
Morey Pond	-	●	●					5	1251	14	6		

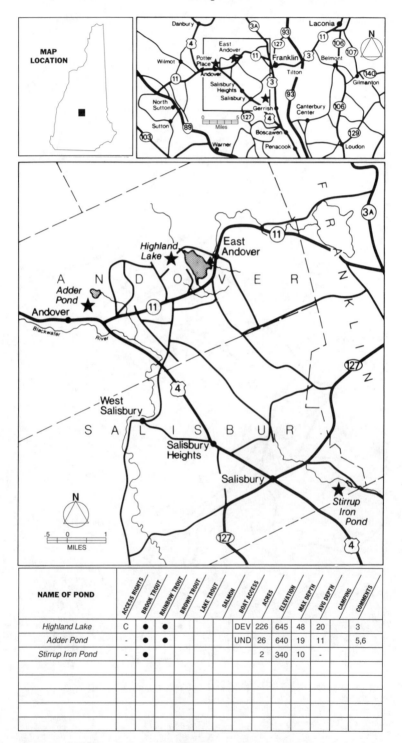

NAME OF POND	ACCESS RIGHTS	BROOK TROUT	RAINBOW TROUT	BROWN TROUT	LAKE TROUT	SALMON	BOAT ACCESS	ACRES	ELEVATION	MAX DEPTH	AVG DEPTH	CAMPING	COMMENTS
Highland Lake	C	●	●				DEV	226	645	48	20		3
Adder Pond	-	●	●				UND	26	640	19	11		5,6
Stirrup Iron Pond	-	●						2	340	10	-		

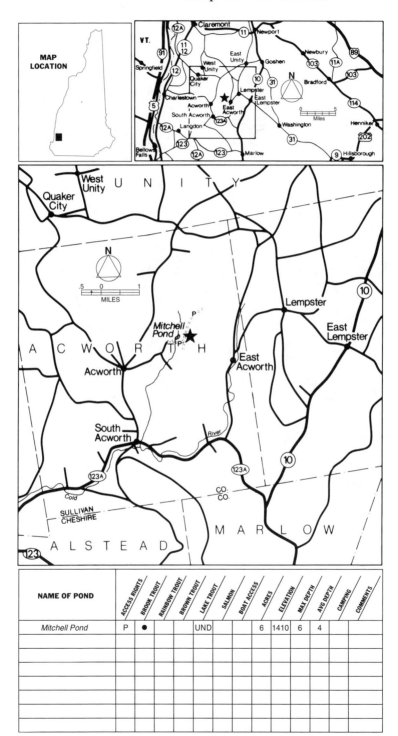

NAME OF POND	ACCESS RIGHTS	BROOK TROUT	RAINBOW TROUT	BROWN TROUT	LAKE TROUT	SALMON	BOAT ACCESS	ACRES	ELEVATION	MAX DEPTH	AVG DEPTH	CAMPING	COMMENTS
Mitchell Pond	P	●			UND			6	1410	6	4		

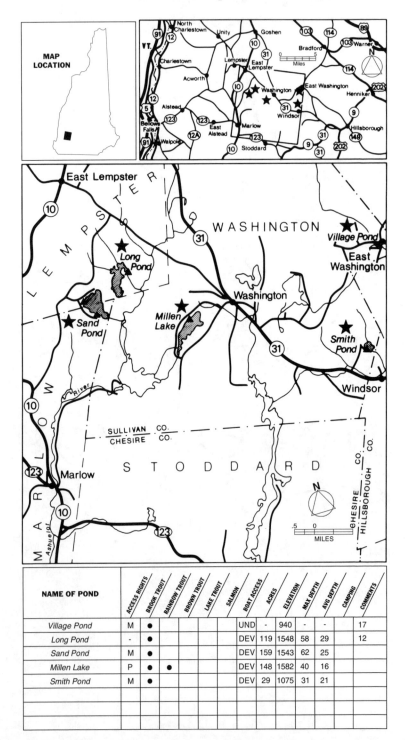

NAME OF POND	ACCESS RIGHTS	BROOK TROUT	RAINBOW TROUT	BROWN TROUT	LAKE TROUT	SALMON	BOAT ACCESS	ACRES	ELEVATION	MAX DEPTH	AVG DEPTH	CAMPING	COMMENTS
Village Pond	M	●					UND	-	940	-	-		17
Long Pond	-	●					DEV	119	1548	58	29		12
Sand Pond	M	●					DEV	159	1543	62	25		
Millen Lake	P	●	●				DEV	148	1582	40	16		
Smith Pond	M	●					DEV	29	1075	31	21		

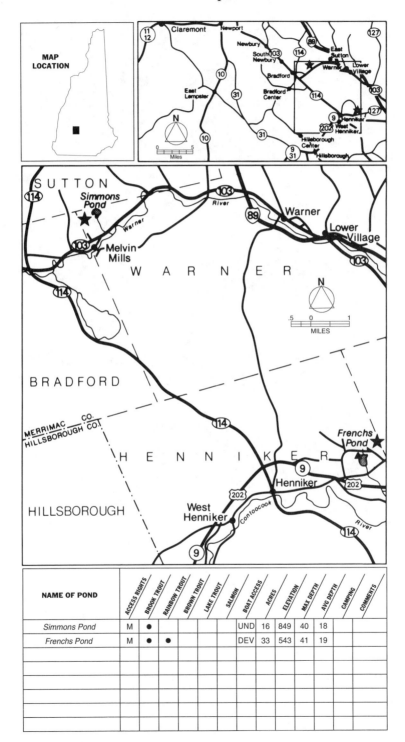

NAME OF POND	ACCESS RIGHTS	BROOK TROUT	RAINBOW TROUT	BROWN TROUT	LAKE TROUT	SALMON	BOAT ACCESS	ACRES	ELEVATION	MAX DEPTH	AVG DEPTH	CAMPING	COMMENTS
Simmons Pond	M	●					UND	16	849	40	18		
Frenchs Pond	M	●	●				DEV	33	543	41	19		

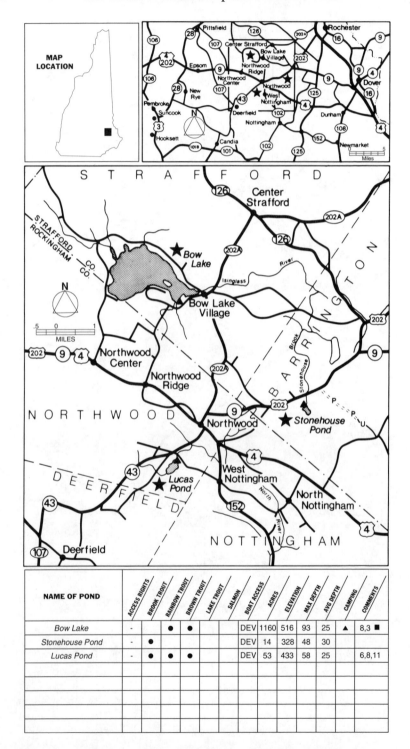

NAME OF POND	ACCESS RIGHTS	BROOK TROUT	RAINBOW TROUT	BROWN TROUT	LAKE TROUT	SALMON	BOAT ACCESS	ACRES	ELEVATION	MAX DEPTH	AVG DEPTH	CAMPING	COMMENTS
Bow Lake	-		●	●			DEV	1160	516	93	25	▲	8,3 ■
Stonehouse Pond	-	●					DEV	14	328	48	30		
Lucas Pond	-	●	●	●			DEV	53	433	58	25		6,8,11

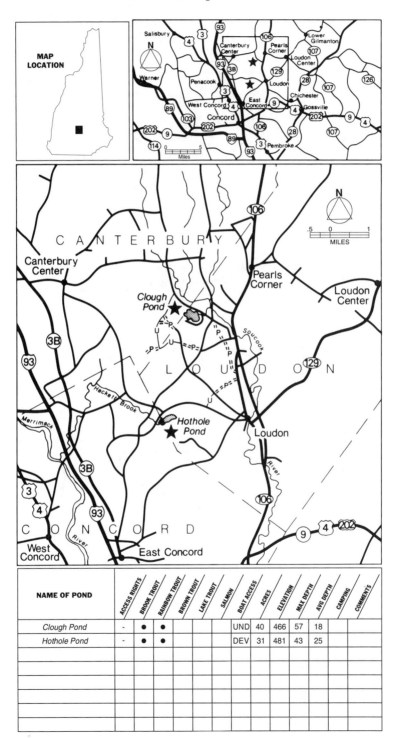

NAME OF POND	ACCESS RIGHTS	BROOK TROUT	RAINBOW TROUT	BROWN TROUT	LAKE TROUT	SALMON	BOAT ACCESS	ACRES	ELEVATION	MAX DEPTH	AVG DEPTH	CAMPING	COMMENTS
Clough Pond	-	●	●				UND	40	466	57	18		
Hothole Pond	-	●	●				DEV	31	481	43	25		

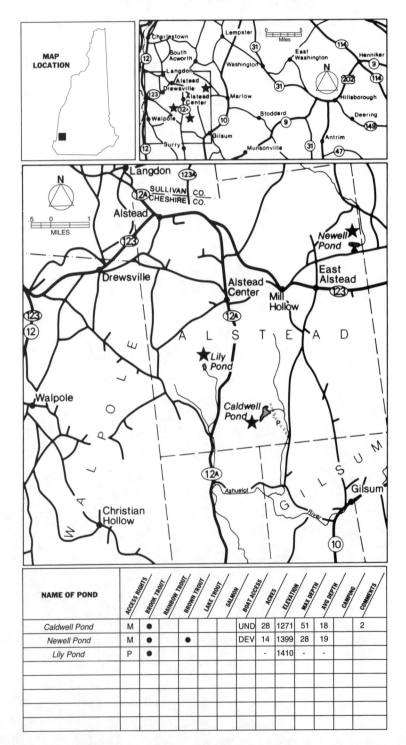

NAME OF POND	ACCESS RIGHTS	BROOK TROUT	RAINBOW TROUT	BROWN TROUT	LAKE TROUT	SALMON	BOAT ACCESS	ACRES	ELEVATION	MAX DEPTH	AVG DEPTH	CAMPING	COMMENTS
Caldwell Pond	M	●					UND	28	1271	51	18		2
Newell Pond	M	●		●			DEV	14	1399	28	19		
Lily Pond	P	●						-	1410	-	-		

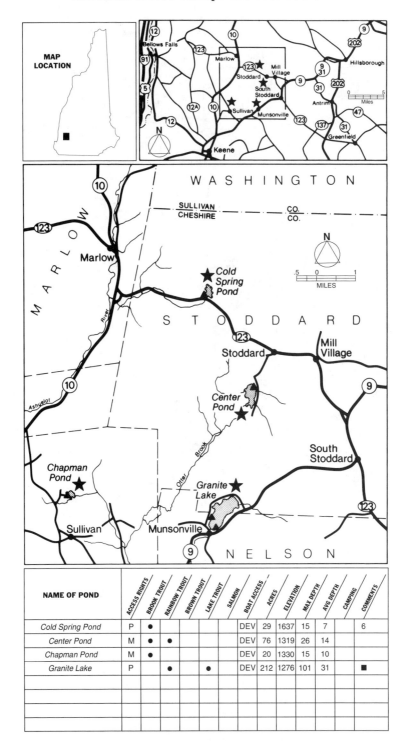

NAME OF POND	ACCESS RIGHTS	BROOK TROUT	RAINBOW TROUT	BROWN TROUT	LAKE TROUT	SALMON	BOAT ACCESS	ACRES	ELEVATION	MAX DEPTH	AVG DEPTH	CAMPING	COMMENTS
Cold Spring Pond	P	●					DEV	29	1637	15	7		6
Center Pond	M	●	●				DEV	76	1319	26	14		
Chapman Pond	M	●					DEV	20	1330	15	10		
Granite Lake	P		●		●		DEV	212	1276	101	31		■

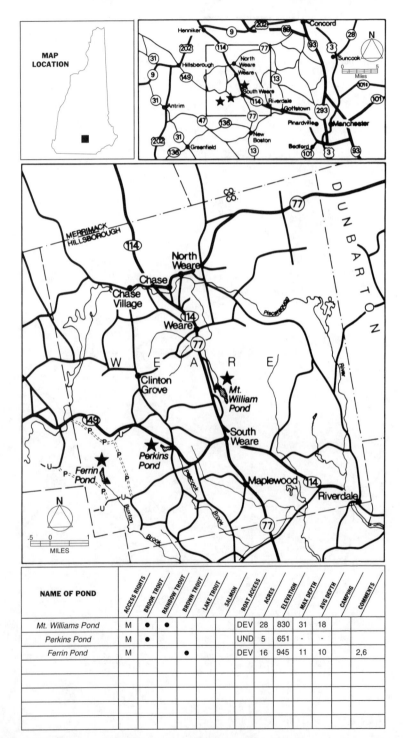

NAME OF POND	ACCESS RIGHTS	BROOK TROUT	RAINBOW TROUT	BROWN TROUT	LAKE TROUT	SALMON	BOAT ACCESS	ACRES	ELEVATION	MAX DEPTH	AVG DEPTH	CAMPING	COMMENTS
Mt. Williams Pond	M	●	●				DEV	28	830	31	18		
Perkins Pond	M	●					UND	5	651	-	-		
Ferrin Pond	M			●			DEV	16	945	11	10		2,6

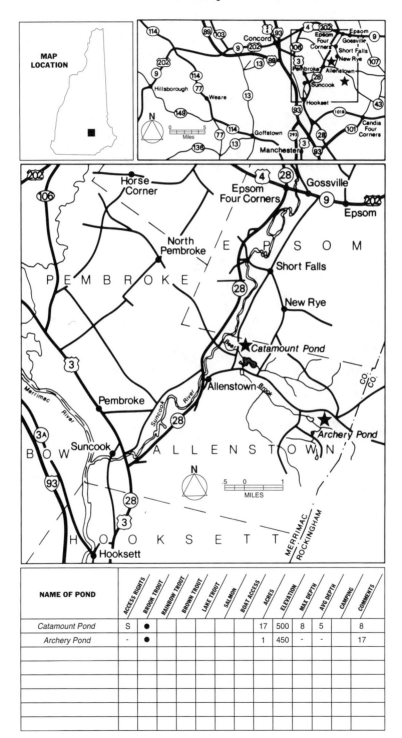

NAME OF POND	ACCESS RIGHTS	BROOK TROUT	RAINBOW TROUT	BROWN TROUT	LAKE TROUT	SALMON	BOAT ACCESS	ACRES	ELEVATION	MAX DEPTH	AVG DEPTH	CAMPING	COMMENTS
Catamount Pond	S	●						17	500	8	5		8
Archery Pond	-	●						1	450	-	-		17

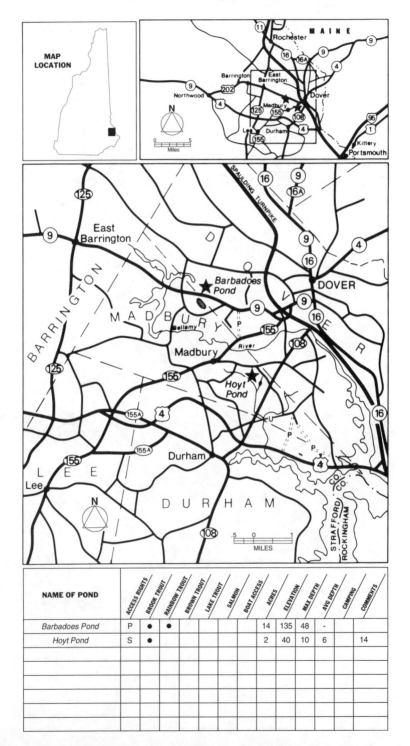

NAME OF POND	ACCESS RIGHTS	BROOK TROUT	RAINBOW TROUT	BROWN TROUT	LAKE TROUT	SALMON	BOAT ACCESS	ACRES	ELEVATION	MAX DEPTH	AVG DEPTH	CAMPING	COMMENTS
Barbadoes Pond	P	●	●					14	135	48	-		
Hoyt Pond	S	●						2	40	10	6		14

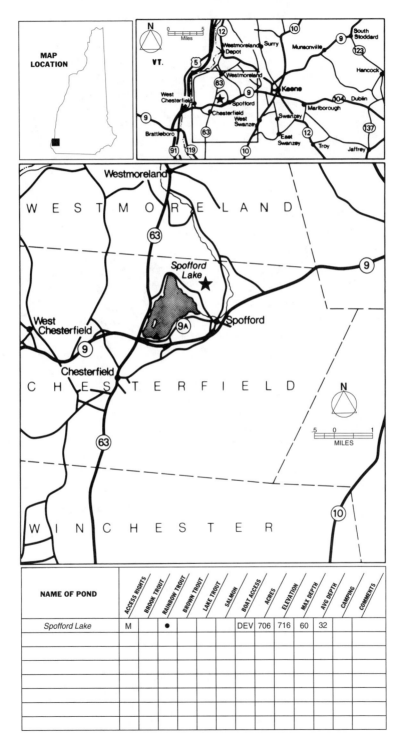

NAME OF POND	ACCESS RIGHTS	BROOK TROUT	RAINBOW TROUT	BROWN TROUT	LAKE TROUT	SALMON	BOAT ACCESS	ACRES	ELEVATION	MAX DEPTH	AVG DEPTH	CAMPING	COMMENTS
Spofford Lake	M		●				DEV	706	716	60	32		

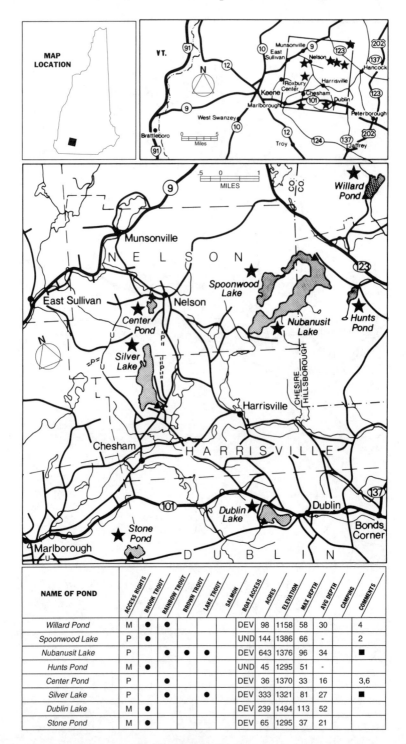

NAME OF POND	ACCESS RIGHTS	BROOK TROUT	RAINBOW TROUT	BROWN TROUT	LAKE TROUT	SALMON	BOAT ACCESS	ACRES	ELEVATION	MAX DEPTH	AVG DEPTH	CAMPING	COMMENTS
Willard Pond	M	●	●				DEV	98	1158	58	30		4
Spoonwood Lake	P	●					UND	144	1386	66	-		2
Nubanusit Lake	P		●	●	●		DEV	643	1376	96	34	■	
Hunts Pond	M	●					UND	45	1295	51	-		
Center Pond	P		●				DEV	36	1370	33	16		3,6
Silver Lake	P		●		●		DEV	333	1321	81	27	■	
Dublin Lake	M	●					DEV	239	1494	113	52		
Stone Pond	M	●					DEV	65	1295	37	21		

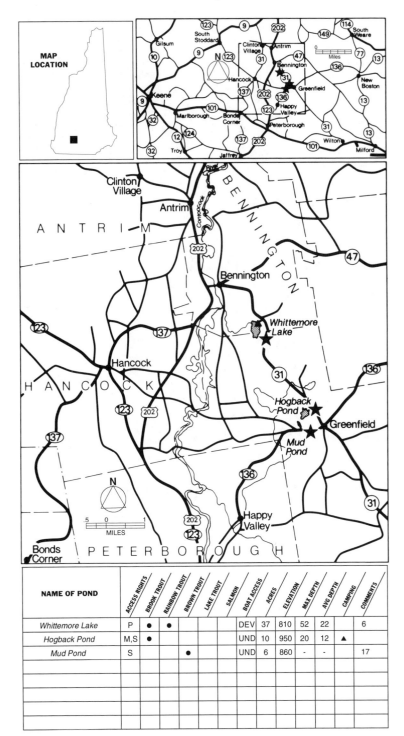

NAME OF POND	ACCESS RIGHTS	BROOK TROUT	RAINBOW TROUT	BROWN TROUT	LAKE TROUT	SALMON	BOAT ACCESS	ACRES	ELEVATION	MAX DEPTH	AVG DEPTH	CAMPING	COMMENTS
Whittemore Lake	P	●	●				DEV	37	810	52	22		6
Hogback Pond	M,S	●					UND	10	950	20	12	▲	
Mud Pond	S			●			UND	6	860	-	-		17

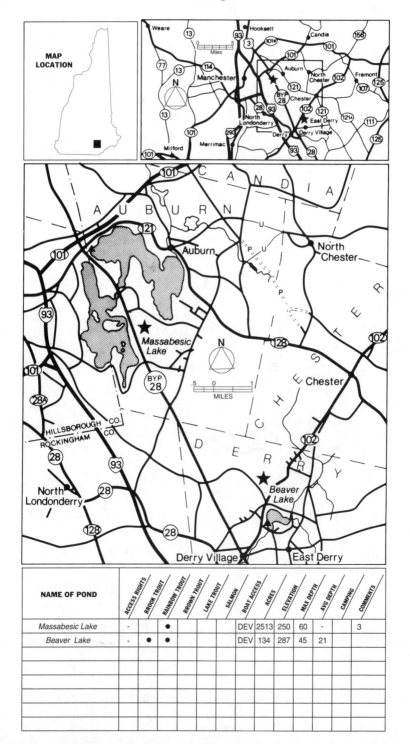

NAME OF POND	ACCESS RIGHTS	BROOK TROUT	RAINBOW TROUT	BROWN TROUT	LAKE TROUT	SALMON	BOAT ACCESS	ACRES	ELEVATION	MAX DEPTH	AVG DEPTH	CAMPING	COMMENTS
Massabesic Lake	-		●				DEV	2513	250	60	-		3
Beaver Lake	-	●	●				DEV	134	287	45	21		

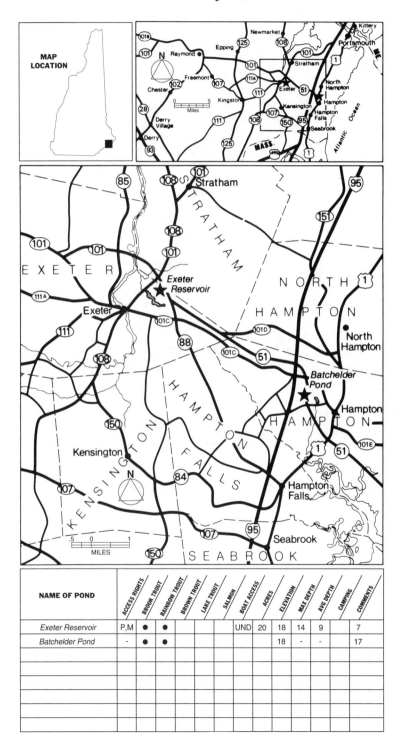

NAME OF POND	ACCESS RIGHTS	BROOK TROUT	RAINBOW TROUT	BROWN TROUT	LAKE TROUT	SALMON	BOAT ACCESS	ACRES	ELEVATION	MAX DEPTH	AVG DEPTH	CAMPING	COMMENTS
Exeter Reservoir	P,M	●	●				UND	20	18	14	9		7
Batchelder Pond	-	●	●						18	-	-		17

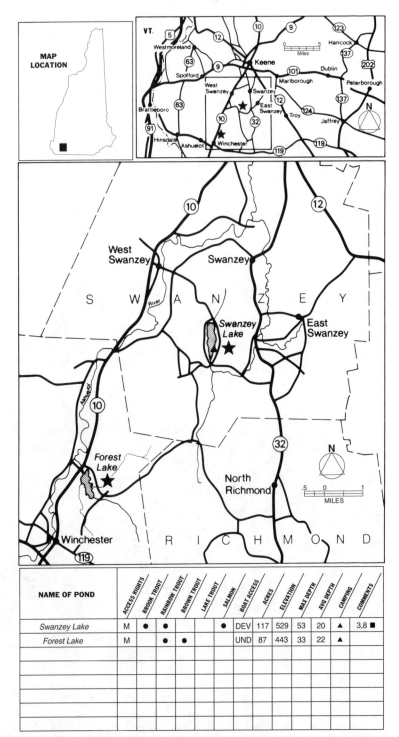

NAME OF POND	ACCESS RIGHTS	BROOK TROUT	RAINBOW TROUT	BROWN TROUT	LAKE TROUT	SALMON	BOAT ACCESS	ACRES	ELEVATION	MAX DEPTH	AVG DEPTH	CAMPING	COMMENTS
Swanzey Lake	M	●	●			●	DEV	117	529	53	20	▲	3,8 ■
Forest Lake	M		●	●			UND	87	443	33	22	▲	

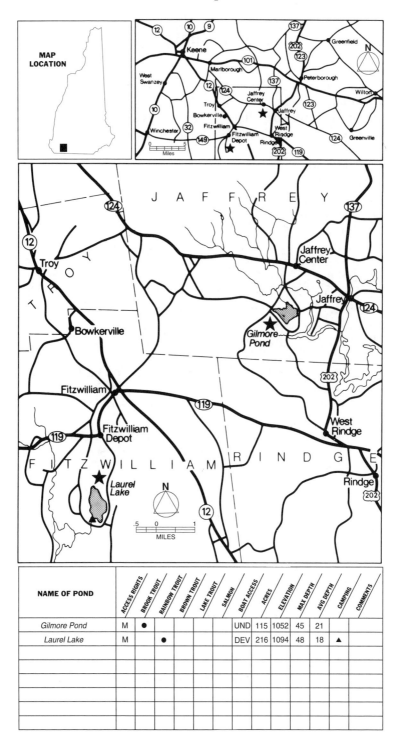

NAME OF POND	ACCESS RIGHTS	BROOK TROUT	RAINBOW TROUT	BROWN TROUT	LAKE TROUT	SALMON	BOAT ACCESS	ACRES	ELEVATION	MAX DEPTH	AVG DEPTH	CAMPING	COMMENTS
Gilmore Pond	M	●					UND	115	1052	45	21		
Laurel Lake	M		●				DEV	216	1094	48	18	▲	

Comments

1. Foot access only, see index for U.S.G.S. Quadrangle(s).
2. Inaccessible by conventional vehicle.
3. Fees charged at some or all accesses.
4. Fly fishing only.
5. No parking.
6. No power boats for outboards.
7. Trail may be difficult to follow.
8. Boat rental.
9. Golden trout.
10. Recommended walk-in, carry a light boat.
11. Tiger trout.
12. Splake.
13. County-owned access.
14. Fish and Game parking lot-walk in ¼ mile.
15. No boats allowed.
16. Multiple boat accesses, fishing excursions.
17. Elevation is approximate.
18. Gate key and boats available for fee, otherwise foot access only.
19. Should be treated as foot access only-some culverts out.
20. The Indian Stream road is accessed from Route U.S. 3 about ¼ mile north of the Indian Stream bridge on U.S. 3.
21. No existing trail.
22. Interstate waters, check regulations.
23. Boat excursion or charter.
24. 44,586 acres.
25. Commercial access is recommended for all but small boats and canoes.
26. North and west sides of this pond are posted.
27. Mud Pond, between Derby and Bryant Ponds, has been recently reclaimed.
28. Remnant brook trout, now managed as warm water.
29. Public access in Maine.
30. Interstate water, check regulations.

Reading Depth Charts

Reading depth charts is not difficult. Readers who are familiar with contour or topographic maps must remember that depth charts show "reverse topography". For readers with no experience in using contour maps it is helpful to understand how they are constructed.

First, sample depth soundings of the lake bottom are made by methodically traversing the lake and recording depth readings with an electronic scanner. These readings are then plotted on a map. See Steps 1 and 2. Points of equal depth are connected by a series of lines called "contour lines". To make the chart less confusing to use, these lines are replaced by "contour intervals", e.g. an interval for every twenty feet of depth. Since it would be only by chance that a sample sounding would be exactly 20, 40 or 60 feet, etc., imaginary points are created. Depths of 20, 40 or 60 feet are interpolated by using known depths and simple arithmetic. Interpolation is methodical guesswork. Accuracy depends on the number of known depths and the distances between them. The size of the contour interval should be appropriate to the size and depth of the lake and the scale of the map. See Steps 3 and 4.

The completed map shows the overall pattern of depths in the lake, the approximate depth at any point in the lake and the gradient of the lake bottom. The farther apart the contour lines, the more gradual is the increase or decrease in depth. Very close contour lines indicate a very steep drop-off or rise in the lake bottom.

The depth charts presented in this book are intended for use in planning a fishing strategy. They are not to be used to purposes of navigation.

Each map includes a profile sketch of the lake bottom based on the contour lines. A profile is created by drawing a straight line (AB) across the lake and graphing

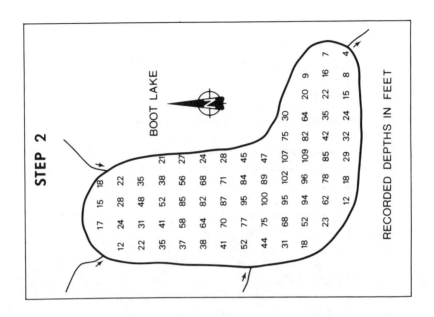

STEP 2

BOOT LAKE

RECORDED DEPTHS IN FEET

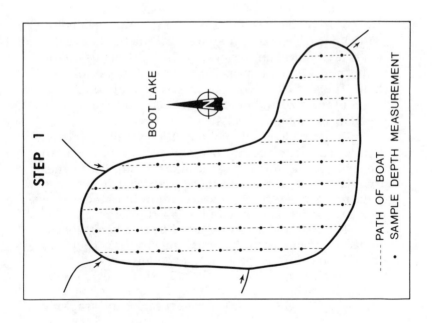

STEP 1

BOOT LAKE

----- PATH OF BOAT

• SAMPLE DEPTH MEASUREMENT

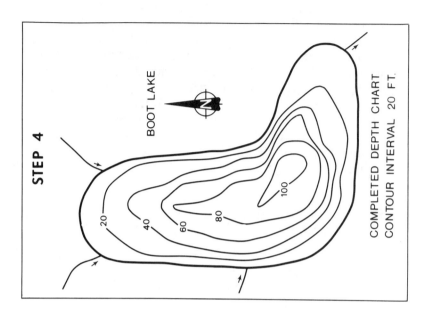

STEP 4

BOOT LAKE

COMPLETED DEPTH CHART
CONTOUR INTERVAL 20 FT.

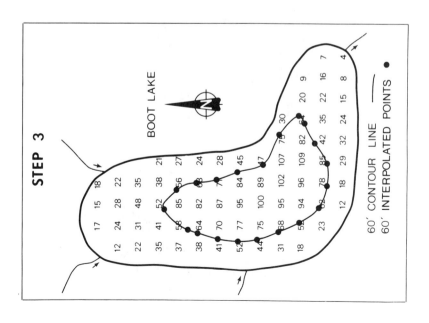

STEP 3

BOOT LAKE

60' CONTOUR LINE ———
60' INTERPOLATED POINTS ●

the intersection of this line where it crosses the contour lines. The profile is determined by where the line is drawn. All the lake bottom profiles in the following charts are based on a line drawn through the deepest part of the lake. These representations will be helpful to readers who are unfamiliar with contour maps. The line selected for the profile is not intended to indicate a desirable trolling route but to assist the reader in creating a mental picture of the bottom along his or her own chosen trolling lane. Comparing several profiles clearly shows the relationship of contours with the lake bottom. These profiles also provide "at-a-glance" insight into the character of the lakes.

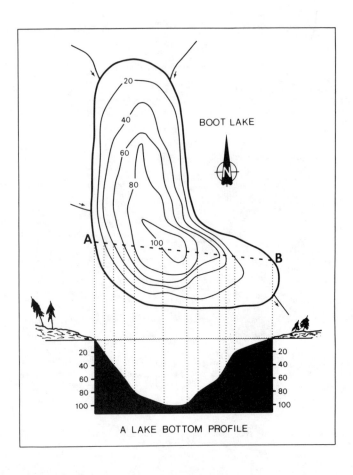

A LAKE BOTTOM PROFILE

LEGEND

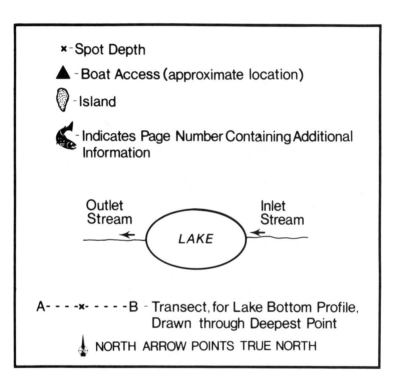

× - Spot Depth

▲ - Boat Access (approximate location)

- Island

- Indicates Page Number Containing Additional Information

Outlet Stream   Inlet Stream

LAKE

A - - - -×- - - - -B - Transect, for Lake Bottom Profile, Drawn through Deepest Point

NORTH ARROW POINTS TRUE NORTH

Maps are not to be used for navigation

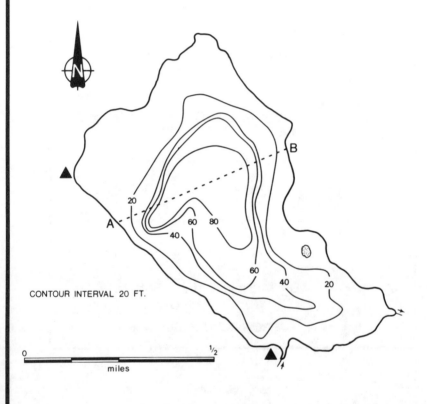

BIG DIAMOND POND
Stewartstown

CONTOUR INTERVAL 20 FT.

20

60 80

40

60

40   20

0   ½
      miles

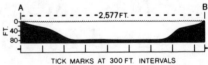

A ──────── 2,577 FT. ──────── B

TICK MARKS AT 300 FT. INTERVALS

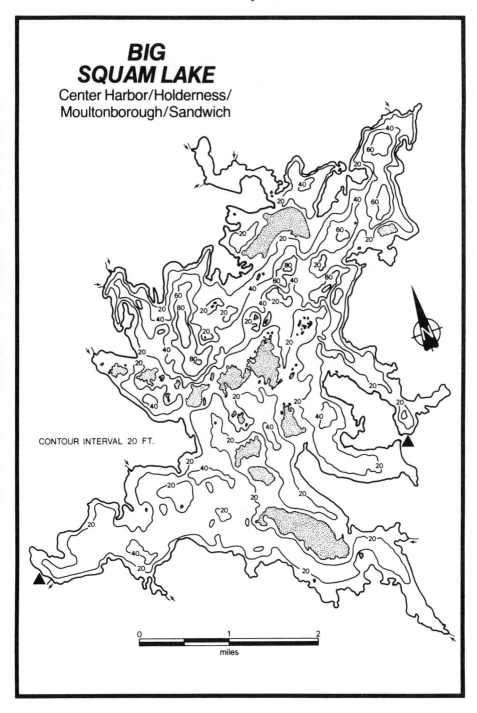

BIG
SQUAM LAKE
Center Harbor/Holderness/
Moultonborough/Sandwich

CONTOUR INTERVAL 20 FT.

0   1   2
miles

FIRST CONNECTICUT LAKE
Pittsburg

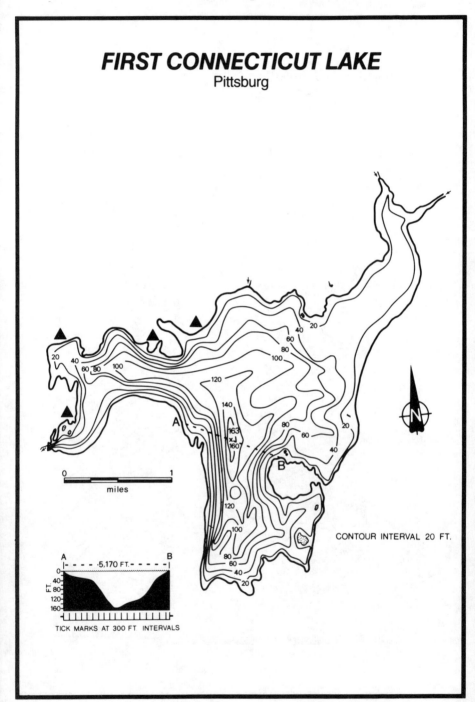

CONTOUR INTERVAL 20 FT.

0 ———————— 1
miles

A ———— 5,170 FT. ———— B

FT.
0
40
80
120
160

TICK MARKS AT 300 FT INTERVALS

GREENOUGH POND

Wentworths Location

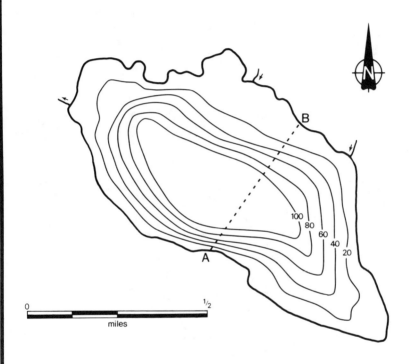

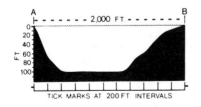

miles

CONTOUR INTERVAL 20 FT.

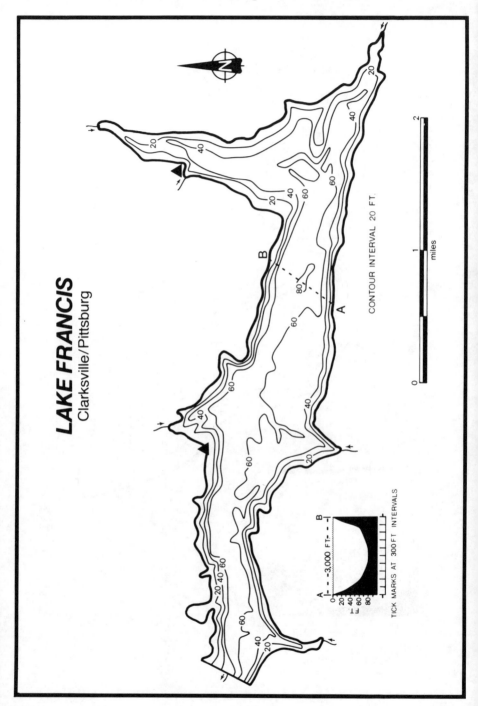

LAKE FRANCIS
Clarksville/Pittsburg

CONTOUR INTERVAL 20 FT.

miles

0   1   2

TICK MARKS AT 300 FT. INTERVALS

A   3,000 FT.   B

0
20
40
60
80
FT.

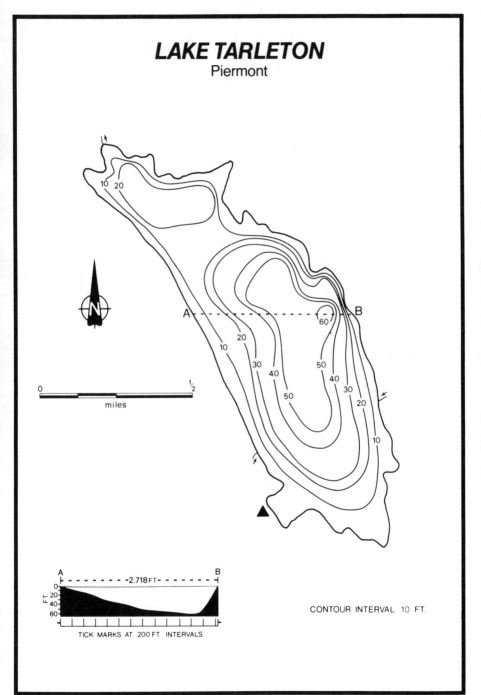

LAKE TARLETON
Piermont

0 _____ 1/2
miles

CONTOUR INTERVAL 10 FT.

A ------- 2,718 FT ------- B

FT

TICK MARKS AT 200 FT INTERVALS

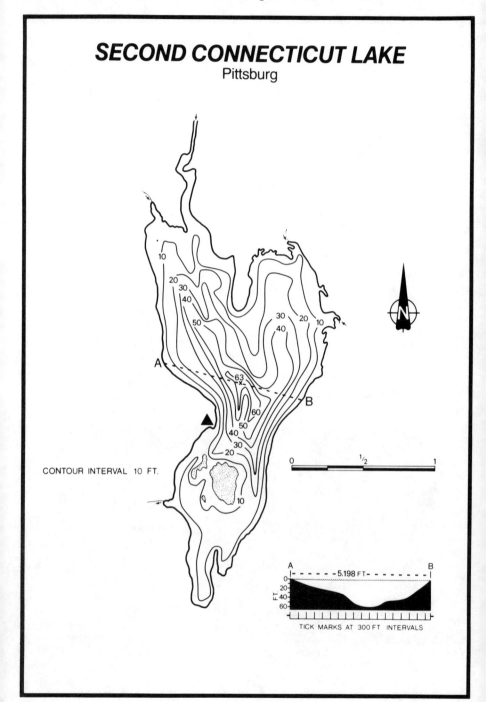

SECOND CONNECTICUT LAKE
Pittsburg

CONTOUR INTERVAL 10 FT.

0   ½   1

A — 5.198 FT. — B

TICK MARKS AT 300 FT INTERVALS

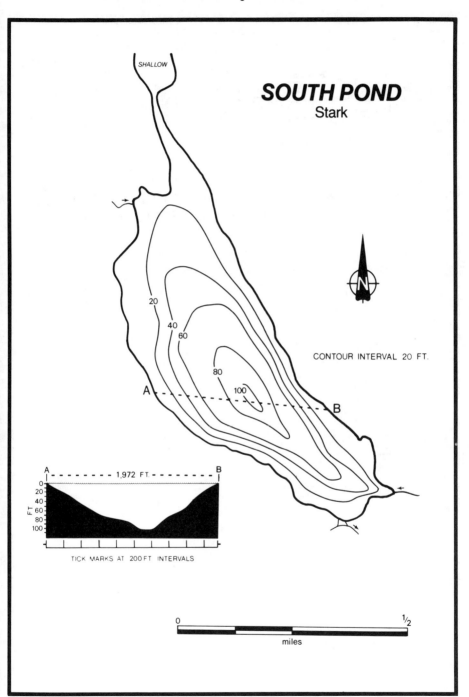

SHALLOW

SOUTH POND
Stark

N

CONTOUR INTERVAL 20 FT.

20

40

60

80

100

A

B

A — 1,972 FT. — B

FT
0
20
40
60
80
100

TICK MARKS AT 200 FT. INTERVALS

0   ½
miles

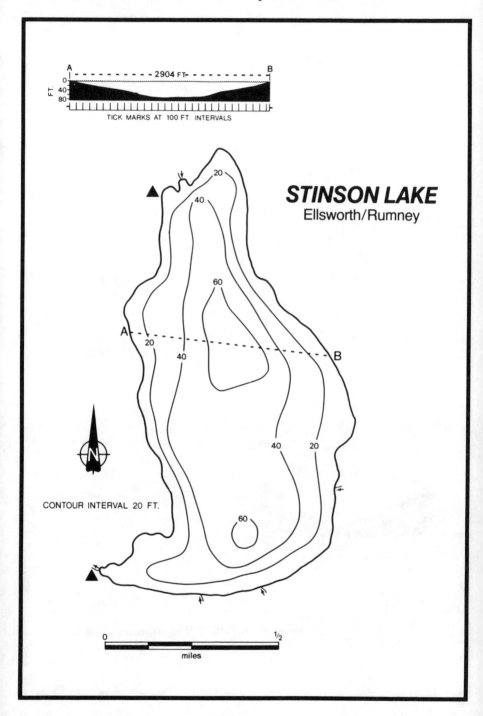

A — — — 2904 FT — — — — B

TICK MARKS AT 100 FT. INTERVALS

STINSON LAKE
Ellsworth/Rumney

CONTOUR INTERVAL 20 FT.

0   ½
miles

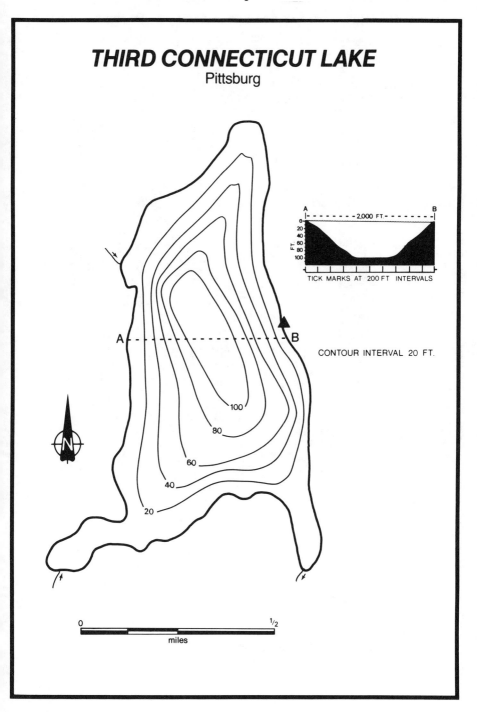

THIRD CONNECTICUT LAKE
Pittsburg

A — — — — — — — — — B

2,000 FT.

TICK MARKS AT 200 FT INTERVALS

CONTOUR INTERVAL 20 FT.

100
80
60
40
20

N

0   ¹/₂
miles

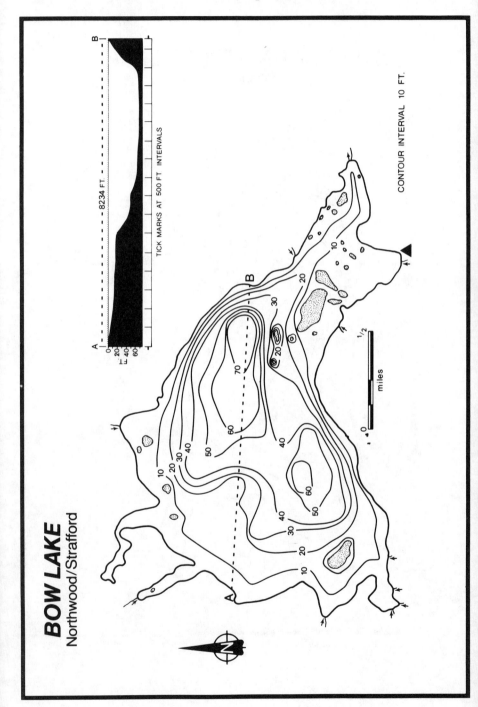

BOW LAKE
Northwood/Strafford

CONTOUR INTERVAL 10 FT.

8234 FT.

TICK MARKS AT 500 FT INTERVALS

miles
1/2

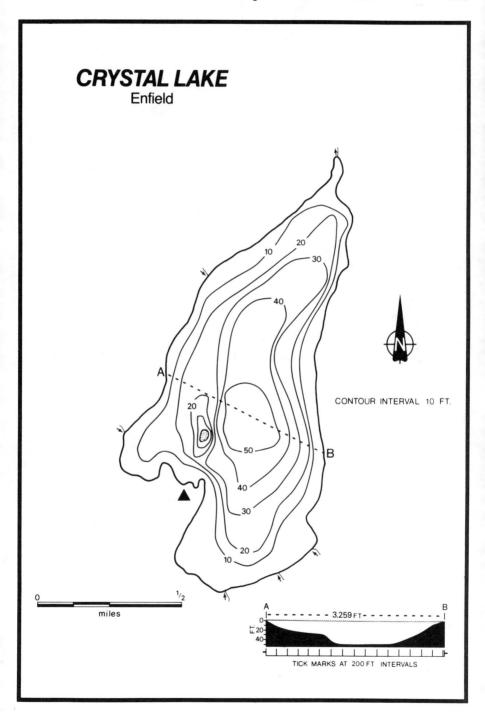

CRYSTAL LAKE
Enfield

CONTOUR INTERVAL 10 FT.

N

0 ____ 1/2
miles

A - - - - - - 3,259 FT - - - - - - B
FT.
TICK MARKS AT 200 FT INTERVALS

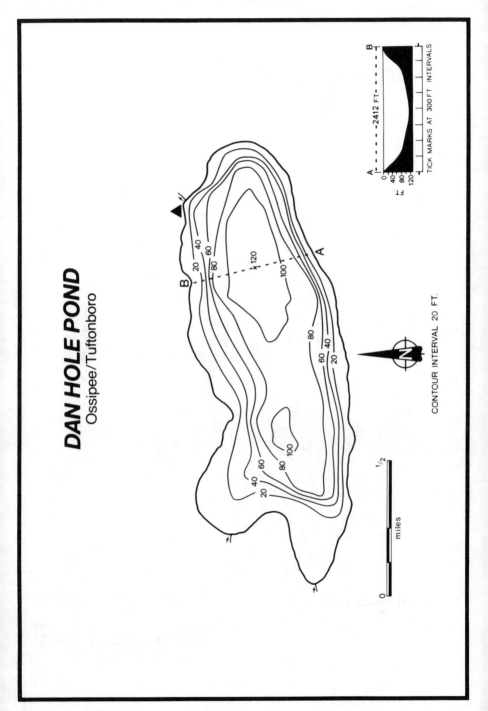

DAN HOLE POND
Ossipee/Tuftonboro

CONTOUR INTERVAL 20 FT.

TICK MARKS AT 300 FT. INTERVALS

-2412 FT-

FT.

miles

GRANITE LAKE
Nelson/Stoddard

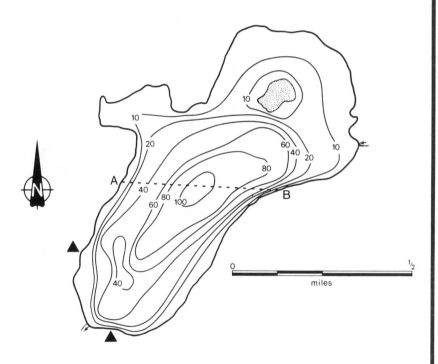

10

10

20

60
40
20

10

80

40
80   100
60

40

N

0   ½

miles

CONTOUR INTERVAL 10 FT.

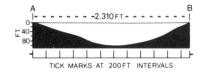

A — — — — –2,310 FT– — — — — B

0
40
80

FT

TICK MARKS AT 200 FT INTERVALS

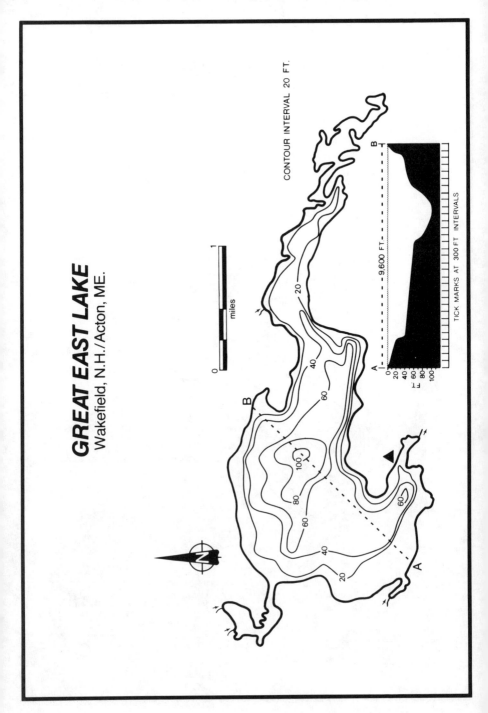

GREAT EAST LAKE
Wakefield, N.H./Acton, ME.

CONTOUR INTERVAL 20 FT.

9,600 FT.

TICK MARKS AT 300 FT INTERVALS

FT.

miles

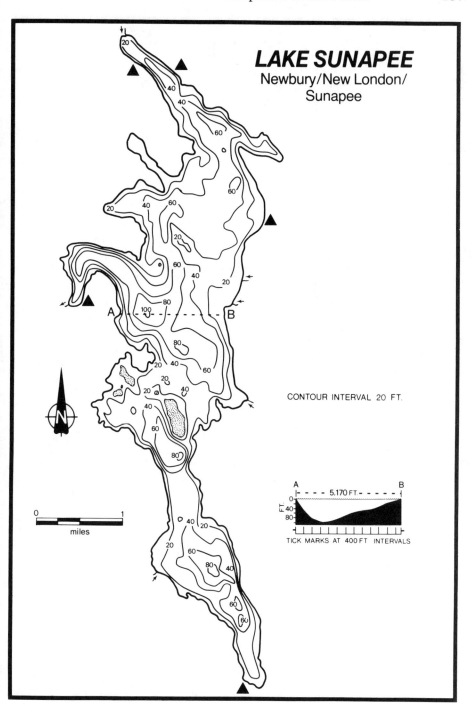

LAKE SUNAPEE
Newbury/New London/
Sunapee

CONTOUR INTERVAL 20 FT.

0   1
miles

N

A   B

A - - - 5.170 FT. - - - - B
FT.
0
40
80

TICK MARKS AT 400 FT INTERVALS

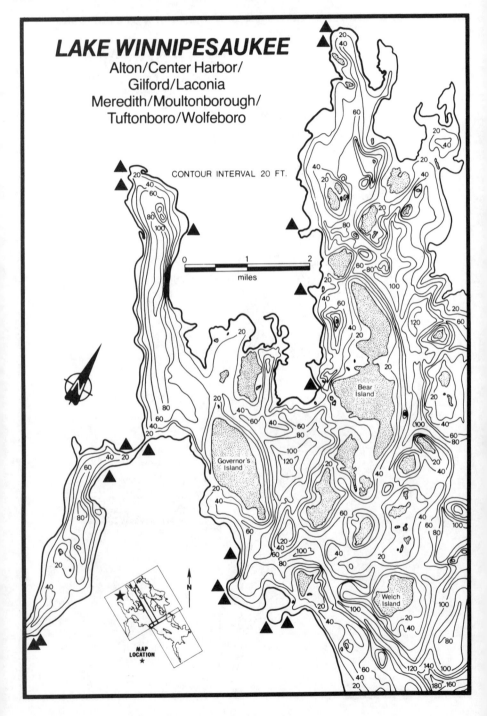

LAKE WINNIPESAUKEE
Alton/Center Harbor/
Gilford/Laconia
Meredith/Moultonborough/
Tuftonboro/Wolfeboro

CONTOUR INTERVAL 20 FT.

0   1   2
miles

Bear
Island

Governor's
Island

Welch
Island

MAP
LOCATION
★

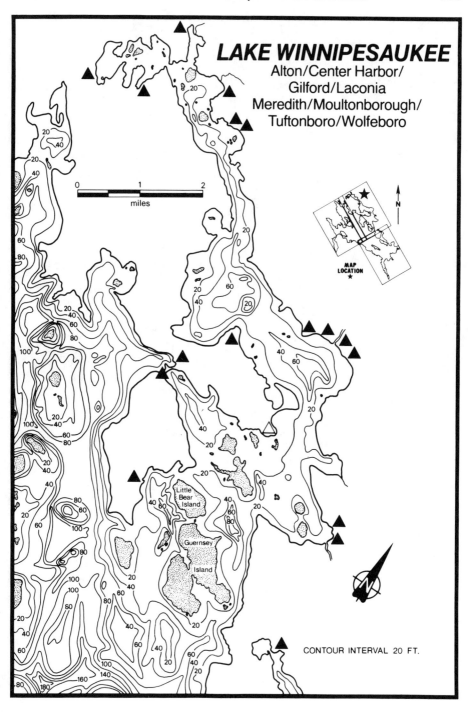

LAKE WINNIPESAUKEE
Alton/Center Harbor/
Gilford/Laconia
Meredith/Moultonborough/
Tuftonboro/Wolfeboro

miles

0 1 2

N

MAP
LOCATION
★

Little
Bear
Island

Guernsey
Island

CONTOUR INTERVAL 20 FT.

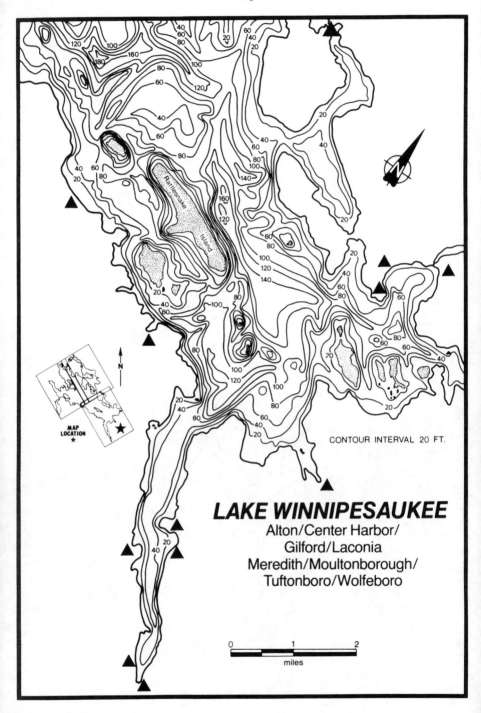

CONTOUR INTERVAL 20 FT.

MAP
LOCATION
★

N

Rattlesnake Island

LAKE WINNIPESAUKEE
Alton/Center Harbor/
Gilford/Laconia
Meredith/Moultonborough/
Tuftonboro/Wolfeboro

0   1   2
miles

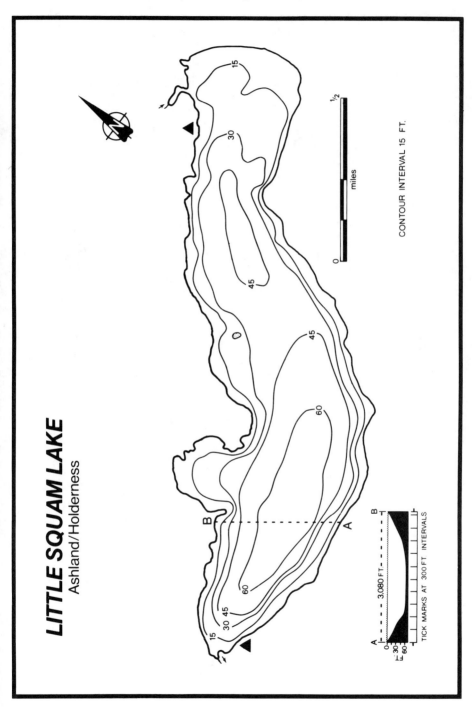

LITTLE SQUAM LAKE
Ashland/Holderness

CONTOUR INTERVAL 15 FT.

miles

15

30

45

45

60

60

45
30
15

3,080 FT

TICK MARKS AT 300 FT INTERVALS

A

B

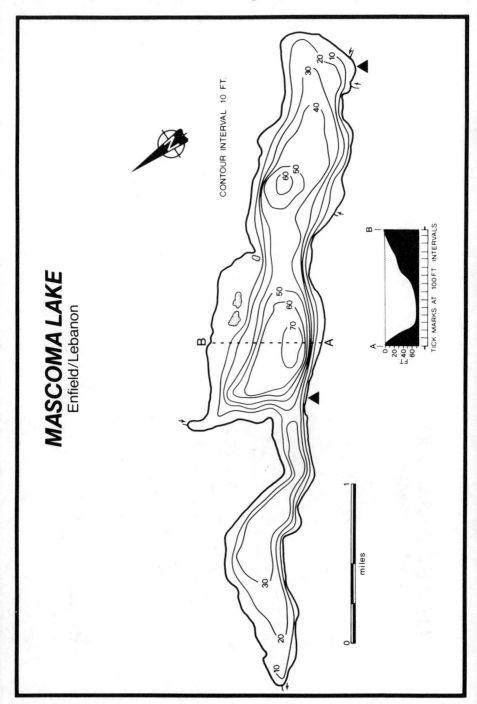

MASCOMA LAKE
Enfield/Lebanon

CONTOUR INTERVAL 10 FT.

TICK MARKS AT 100FT INTERVALS

miles

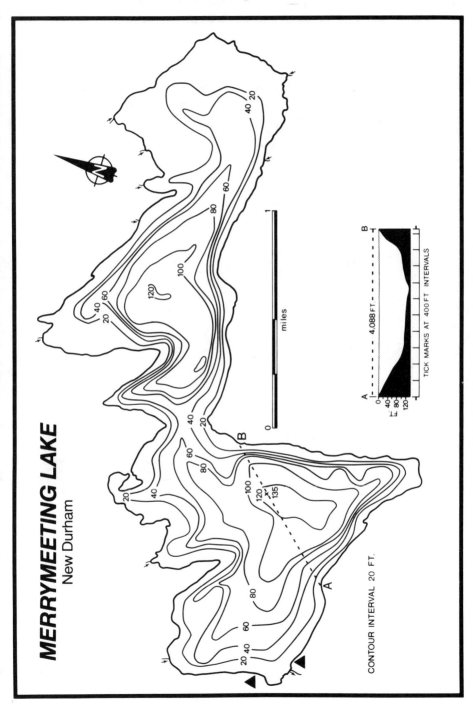

MERRYMEETING LAKE
New Durham

miles

CONTOUR INTERVAL 20 FT.

4,088 FT

TICK MARKS AT 400 FT INTERVALS

FT.

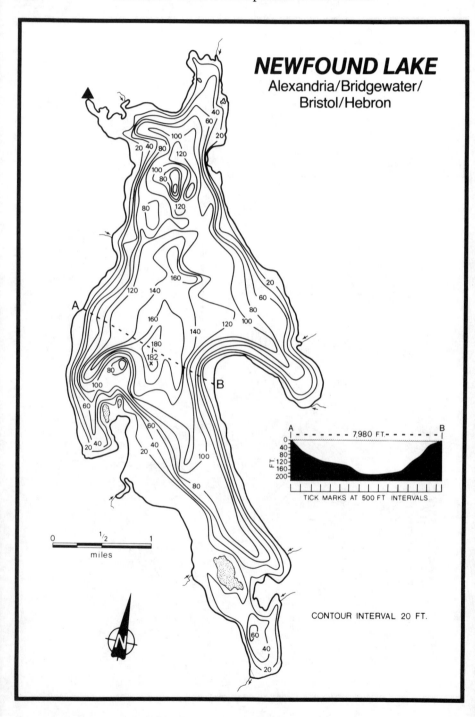

NEWFOUND LAKE
Alexandria/Bridgewater/
Bristol/Hebron

A ─── 7,980 FT ─── B

TICK MARKS AT 500 FT INTERVALS

CONTOUR INTERVAL 20 FT.

0   1/2   1
miles

NUBANUSIT LAKE
Hancock/Nelson

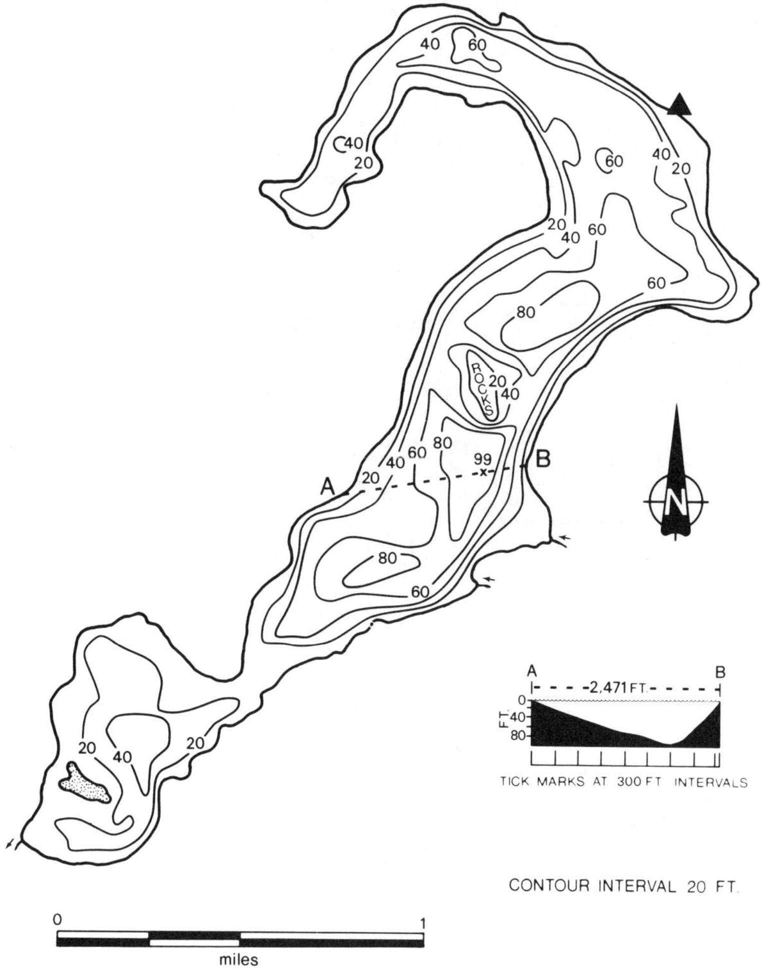

40 60

C40
20

60 40
20

20
40 60

60

80

ROCKS 20
40

80
40 60 99
A 20 x B

80
60

20 40 20

A - - -2,471 FT.- - - B
0
FT. 40
80
TICK MARKS AT 300 FT INTERVALS

N

CONTOUR INTERVAL 20 FT.

0 1
miles

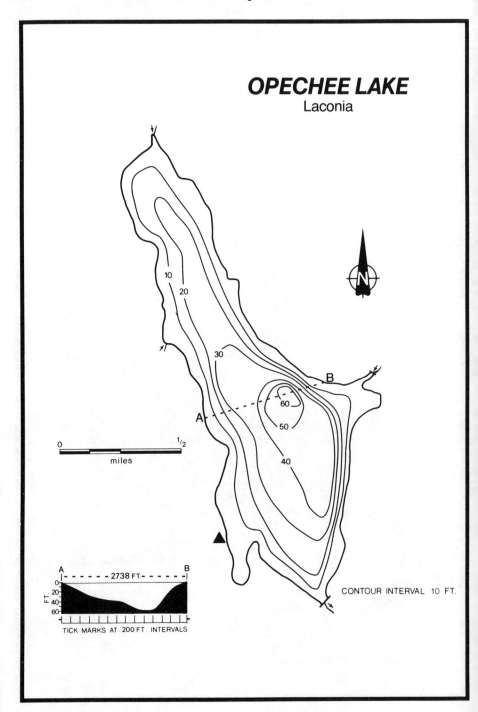

OPECHEE LAKE
Laconia

N

10
20
30
B
60
A
50
40

0   1/2
miles

CONTOUR INTERVAL 10 FT.

A   B
- - - - 2738 FT. - - - -
FT
0
20
40
60
TICK MARKS AT 200 FT INTERVALS

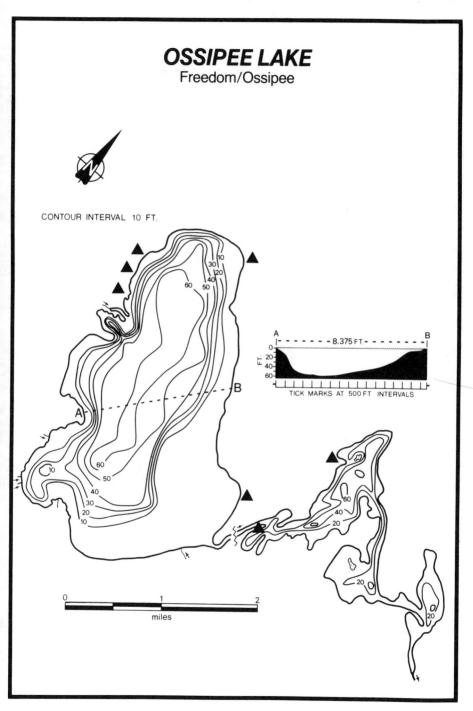

OSSIPEE LAKE
Freedom/Ossipee

CONTOUR INTERVAL 10 FT.

A — — — 8.375 FT — — — B
FT.
TICK MARKS AT 500 FT INTERVALS

0   1   2
miles

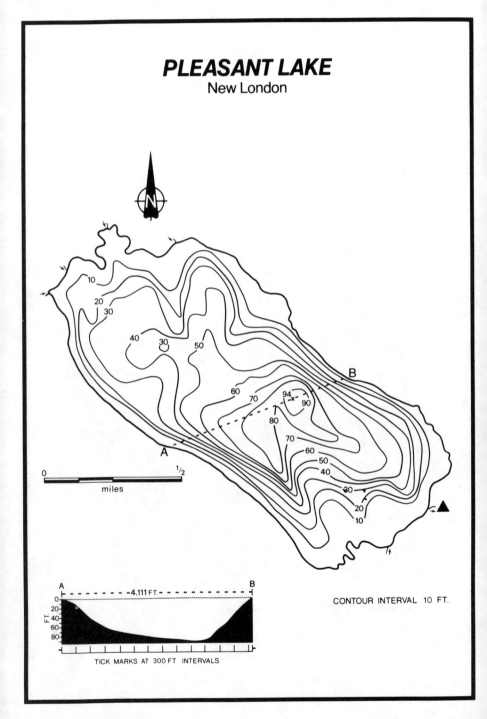

PLEASANT LAKE
New London

CONTOUR INTERVAL 10 FT.

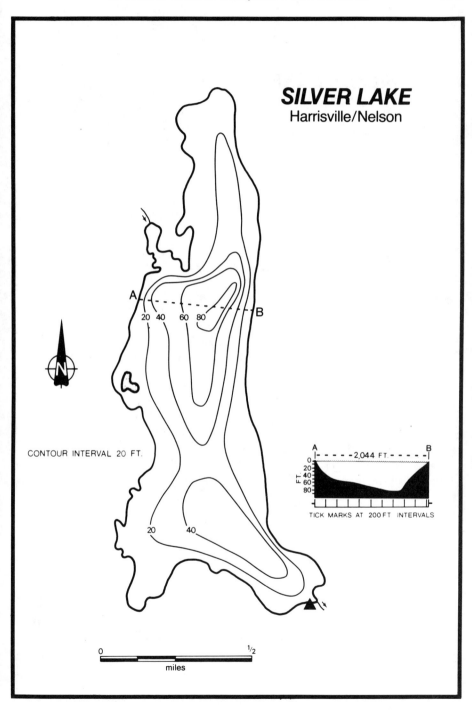

SILVER LAKE
Harrisville/Nelson

A 20 40 60 80 B

CONTOUR INTERVAL 20 FT.

N

20 40

A ---- 2,044 FT. ---- B
0
20
40
FT. 60
80
TICK MARKS AT 200 FT. INTERVALS

0   1/2
miles

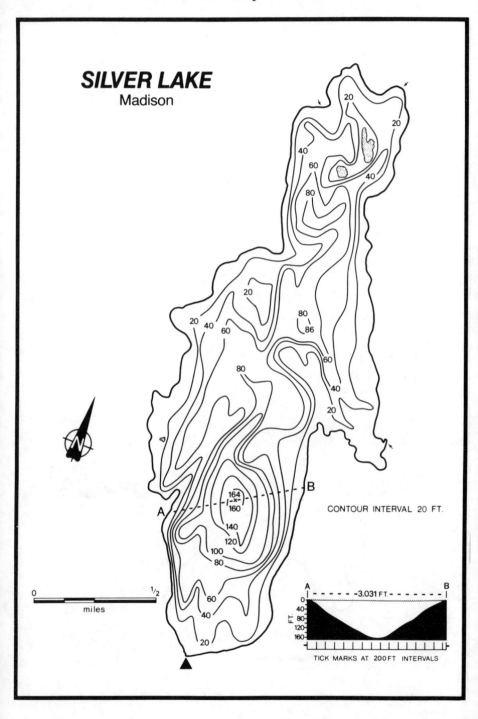

SILVER LAKE
Madison

CONTOUR INTERVAL 20 FT.

0   1/2
miles

A — — — — 3,031 FT. — — — — B

TICK MARKS AT 200 FT INTERVALS

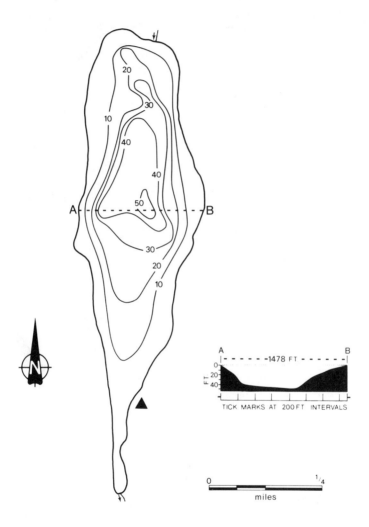

SWANZEY LAKE
Swanzey

A - - - - - -1478 FT - - - - - B

TICK MARKS AT 200 FT INTERVALS

0   1/4
miles

CONTOUR INTERVAL 10 FT.

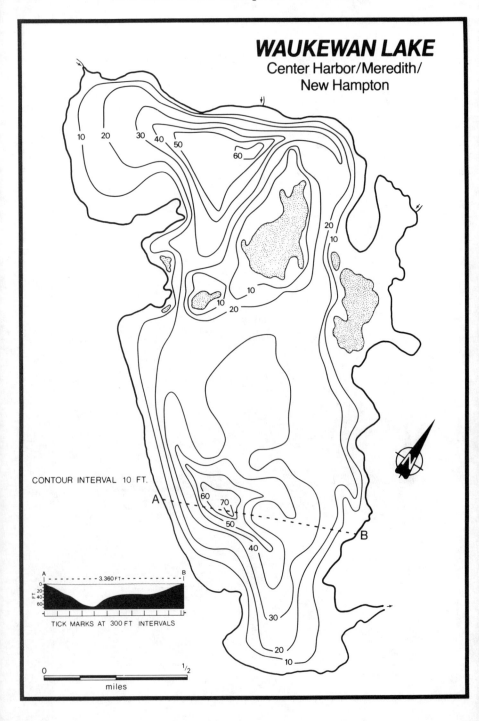

WAUKEWAN LAKE
Center Harbor/Meredith/
New Hampton

CONTOUR INTERVAL 10 FT.

A — — — 3.360 FT — — — — B

TICK MARKS AT 300 FT INTERVALS

0   1/2

miles

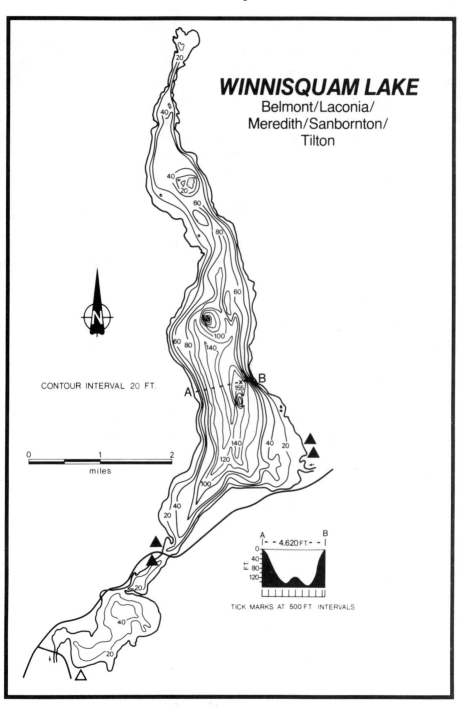

WINNISQUAM LAKE
Belmont/Laconia/
Meredith/Sanbornton/
Tilton

N

CONTOUR INTERVAL 20 FT.

0   1   2
miles

A   B
- - 4,620 FT- -

FT.
0
40
80
120

TICK MARKS AT 500 FT INTERVALS

Bibliography

Alphabetical Listings of Water Resources. New
Hampshire Water Resources Board. 1981.

*Area of Water Bodies in the State of New
Hampshire.* An Inventory Prepared by the New
Hampshire State Planning Board. Concord,
New Hampshire. 1934.

Bergman, Ray. *Trout.* Second Edition. Alfred A.
Knopf. 1972.

Bulletin of American Meteorological Society. June
1982. pp.598-618. (An overview of acid rain
programs).

Cowing, Derril J. and Douglas Lash.
*Characteristics of Lakes, Ponds and Reservoirs
of New Hampshie, with a Bibliography.*
U.S.G.S. Open File Report 75-490, June 1975.
Prepared in cooperation with New Hampshire
Water Supply and Pollution Control
Commission. (Computer print-out with
extensive bibliography on the State's water
bodies, held at the State Library, Concord,
New Hampshire) 1975.

Disley, John. *Orienteering.* Stackpole Books.
Harrisburg, Pennsylvania. 1967. (For the
would-be bushwhacker, this is an introduction
to map and compass work.)

Doan, Daniel. *Fifty Hikes In New Hampshire's
White Mountains.* New Hampshire Publishing
Company. Somersworth, New Hampshire,
1977.

Doan, Daniel. *Fifty More Hikes in New
Hampshire.* New Hampshire Publishing
Company. Somersworth, New Hampshire.
1978.

Fishing On the White Mountain National Forest.
U.S. Department of Agriculture. (Pamphlet, no
date.)

1982 Freshwater/Marine Fishing Seasons. New
Hampshire Fish and Game Department.
(Everyone needs to read this annual edition of
rules and regulations.)

Goldthwait, James Walter. *The Geology of New
Hampshire.* New Hampshire Academy of
Science, Handbook No. 1, Rumford Press,
Concord, New Hampshire. (Classic work on
glaciation.) 1925.

Greenhood, David. *Mapping.* The University of
Chicago Press. Chicago and London. 1964.

*Guide to the Appalachian Trail in New Hampshire
and Vermont. Third Edition.* The Appalachian
Trail Conference. Harpers Ferry, West Virginia.
1979.

*Inventory of Outdoor Recreation Facilities. New
Hampshire Office of State Planning,* Ronald
Poltak, Director. Century House. Watkins
Glen, New York. (Comprehensive inventory
and maps of a variety of recreational features -
made available through the New Hampshire
Historical Society.) 1981.

Jorgensen, Neil. *A Guide to New England's
Landscape.* Barre Publishers. Barre, Vermont.
1971.

McClane, A.J. *McClane's New Standard Fishing
Encyclopedia and International Angling Guide.*
Holt, Rinehart and Winston. 1974.

*New Hampshire Boating Laws, Rules and
Regulations.* Department of Safety, Division of
Safety Services. (Published periodically).

New Hampshire Camping Guide. New Hampshire
Division of Economic Development and New
Hampshire Campground Owners' Association.
1981.

New Hampshire Code of Administrative Rules. Part Fis 405.01 Lake Trout Lakes; Part Fis 405.04 Reclaimed Trout Ponds; Part Fis 405.03 Trout Ponds.

New Hampshire Water Bodies and Public Access Points, 1964 - Data Book. New Hampshire State Planning Project: Land-Water-Recreation, Report No. 4. 1964.

Northern New England Zebra Mussel Watch. University of New Hampshire. Sea Grant/ Cooperative Extension. (No date).

Power Boat Restrictions. Promulgated under RSA 486 and RSA 270:12. State of New Hampshire, Department of Safety. (No date).

Safe Boating in New Hampshire. New Hampshire Department of Safety. (No date).

Scarola, John F. *Freshwater Fishes of New Hampshire.* New Hampshire Fish and Game Department. 1973. (Excellent colorful book on New Hampshire's fish.)

State of New Hampshire: General Highway Maps. County Series. New Hampshire Department of Public Works and Highways. Planning and Economic Division. (Various dates.)

Stocking Records. New Hampshire Fish and Game Department. 1981.

U.S. Geological Survey. Selected quadrangles.

Water Milfoil. Environmental Fact Sheet, NHDES Technical Bulletin WSPCD-1989-1. New Hampshire Department of Environmental Services.

White Mountain National Forest, New Hampshire-Maine. (Map). U.S. Department of Agriculture. 1972.

Pond Index

Long Pond, Lempster, 100
Long Pond, Millsfield, 56
Loon Lake, 82
Lost Pond, 63
Lower Carter Pond, 63, see U.S.G.S. Quadrangle
    Carter Dome, 7.5"
Lower Greeley Pond, 69, see U.S.G.S. Quadrangle
    Mt. Osceola, 7.5"
Lower Hall Pond, 77
Lower Mountain Pond, 62
Lower Three Ponds, 75, see U.S.G.S. Quadrangle
    Mount Kineo, 7.5"
Lucas Pond, 102
Martin Meadow Pond, 60
Mascoma Lake, 89
Massabesic Lake, 112
Merrymeeting Lake, 94
Middle Pond, 48
Middle Hall Pond, 77, see U.S.G.S. Quadrangle
    Squam Mountains, 7.5"
Middle Three Ponds, 75, see U.S.G.S. Quadrangle
    Mount Kineo, 7.5"
Millen Lake, 100
Millsfield Pond, 56
Mirror Lake, 60
Mitchell Pond, 99
Moody Pond, 81
Moore Reservoir, 62
Moose Pond, Millsfield, 57
Moose Pond, Pittsburg, 48
Morey Pond, 97
Mountain Pond, 70, see U.S.G.S. Quadrangle
    Chatham, 7.5"
Mt. Williams Pond, 106
Mud Pond, Dixville, 49, see U.S.G.S. Quadrangle
    Lake Francis, 7.5"
Mud Pond, Easton, 67
Mud Pond, Greenfield, 111
Mud Pond, Lyme, 74, see U.S.G.S. Quadrangle
    Smarts Mountain, 7.5"